America's Greatest Brands

AN INSIGHT INTO MANY OF AMERICA'S STRONGEST AND MOST VALUABLE BRANDS
VOLUME XII

CEO & Publisher
Carl Meyer

President, Superbrands Ltd.
Stephen P. Smith

Managing Editor
Bob Land

Design Director
Jack Huber

Director
Lesley Meyer

Brand Video Services
Jason Smith

Copyright 2000–2017
Superbrands Ltd.

Published by America's Greatest Brands (US) LLC
under license to Superbrands Ltd.
P.O. Box 1
6 Green Pastures Lane
Kent, CT 06757

Telephone (860) 927-3200
Facsimile (860) 927-3228
www.americasgreatestbrands.com

Special thanks to:
Stephen Smith, Luke Johnson, Richard Thomas, Peter Ledbetter, Mark Farrer-Brown, Ben Redmond, John Russell,
Peter Smith, Diane Linley, Jonathan Bond, Michael Capiraso, James Gregory, Rich Jernstedt, Linda Kaplan Thaler,
Michael Mohamad, Keith Reinhard, Kevin Roberts, Antony Young, Megan Whitfield, Agnes, Daniel, Jake Wilson

Additional thanks to: Peter Choy, Ming Lee, Joseph So, and World Print Ltd.; William Wong, Marine Lee, and
OCRA Ltd.; and Infotree Web Services

In Memory of Rohinton Maloo

ISBN 978-0-9899790-2-3

America's Greatest Brands

AN INSIGHT INTO MANY OF AMERICA'S STRONGEST AND MOST VALUABLE BRANDS
VOLUME XII

This book is dedicated to the
men and women who build and protect
America's greatest brand assets.

AWARDED
America's
Greatest Brands
2017

www.americasgreatestbrands.com

CONTENTS

AECOM
1999 Avenue of the Stars
Suite 2600
Los Angeles, CA 90067
aecom.com

Alka-Seltzer
Bayer Healthcare–Consumer Care
Division
36 Colombia Road
Morristown, NJ 07962
consumercare.bayer.com

Andersen Corporation
Andersen Corporation
100 Fourth Avenue North
Bayport, MN 55003
andersenwindows.com

Annin Flags
Annin Flagmakers
105 Eisenhower Parkway
Suite 203
Roseland, NJ 07068
Annin.com

Arrow
PVH Corp.
200 Madison Avenue
New York, NY 10016
pvh.com

AXA Equitable
AXA Equitable Life Insurance Company
1290 Avenue of the Americas
New York, NY 10104
axa-equitable.com

Baskin Robbins
Dunkin' Brands Inc.
130 Royall Street
Canton, MA 02021
dunkinbrands.com

Big Brothers Big Sisters
Big Brothers Big Sisters of America
2202 North Westshore Boulevard
Suite 453
Tampa, FL 33607
bbbs.org

Campbell Soup
Campbell's Soup Company
1 Campbell Place
Camden, NJ 08103
campbellsoup.com

Crayola
Crayola LLC
1100 Church Lane
Easton, PA 18044
crayola.com

Crest
The Procter & Gamble Company
1 Procter & Gamble Plaza
Cincinnati, OH 45202
crest.com

Denny's
Denny's Inc.
203 East Main Street
Spartanburg, SC 29319
dennys.com

Dunkin' Donuts
Dunkin Brands Inc.
130 Royall Street
Canton, MA 02021
dunkinbrands.com

FedEx
Federal Express Corporation
942 South Shady Grove Road
Memphis, TN 38120
fedex.com/us

Hartz Mountain
The Hartz Mountain Corporation
400 Plaza Drive
Secaucus, NJ 07094
hartz.com

Izod
PVH Corp.
200 Madison Avenue
New York NY 10016
pvh.com

Konica Minolta
Konica Minolta Business Solutions,
USA Inc.
101 Williams Drive
Ramsey, NJ 07446
kmbs.konicaminolta.us

Land O'Lakes
Land O'Lakes Inc.
4001 Lexington Avenue North
Arden Hills, MN 55126
landolakesinc.com

Major League Baseball

Major League Baseball

245 Park Avenue

New York, NY 10167

mlb.com

Martinelli

S. Martinelli & Company

P.O. Box 1868

Watsonville, CA 95077

martinellis.com

Martin Guitars

C. F. Martin & Co. Inc.

510 Sycamore Street

Nazareth, PA 18064

martinguitars.com

Mayflower

Unigroup Inc.

1 Premier Drive

Fenton, MO 63026

unigroupinc.com

McCormick

McCormick & Company Inc.

18 Loveton Circle

Sparks, MD 21152

mccormick.com

NCR

NCR Corporation

3097 Satellite Boulevard

Duluth, GA 30096

ncr.com

Oreo

Kraft Foods Inc.

3 Lakes Drive

Northfield, IL 60093

kraft.com

Philadelphia Contributionship

The Philadelphia Contributionship

210 South Fourth Street

Philadelphia, PA 19106

contributionship.com

Rawlings

Rawlings Sporting Goods Company Inc.

510 Maryville University Drive

St. Louis, MO 63141

rawlings.com

See's Candies

See's Candies Inc.

210 El Camino Real

South San Francisco, CA 94080

sees.com

Sun-Maid

Sun-Maid Growers

13525 South Bethel Avenue

Kingsburg, CA 93631

sunmaid.com

Tata Consultancy Services

Tata Group

101 Park Avenue

Floor 26

New York, NY 10178

tcs.com

Tetley Tea

Tata Global Beverages

155 Chestnut Ridge Road

Montvale, NJ 07645

northamerica.tata.com

The New York Times

The New York Times Company

620 Eighth Avenue

New York, NY 10018

nytco.com

United Van Lines

Unigroup Inc.

1 Premier Drive

Fenton, MO 63026

unigroupinc.com

Van Heusen

PVH Corp.

200 Madison Avenue

New York, NY 10016

pvh.com

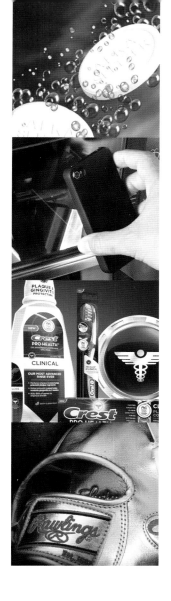

FOREWORD

"To meet demand, brands have to remain fresh and innovative — even while adhering strictly to their core values — and consumer loyalty to those brands over time fuels success."

I n our 12th edition, we at America's Greatest Brands are thrilled to share with you a collection of strong brands that have consistently remained favorite choices of American consumers. These brands all have fascinating stories to tell. This edition also pays tribute to America's great classic brands that are still going strong 100 years and more into their corporate histories.

The relationship between consumers and their brand choices presents an ongoing challenge that involves navigating time and societal changes as well as all the other variables that go into a buyer's decision. To meet demand, brands have to remain fresh and innovative — even while adhering strictly to their core values — and consumer loyalty to those brands over time fuels success. Nothing says success more than forging strong relationships with consumers generation after generation.

Lesley Meyer

Director

*A Strong Brand Identity
Is More Crucial Today
Than Ever Before*

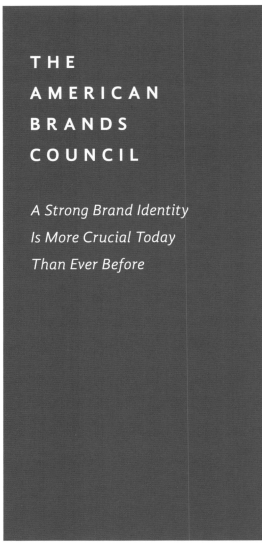

**Jonathan Bond
Chief Executive
Officer, Big Fuel**

Brands used to be all about finding that one unique rational product attribute and hammering away at it. Today the great brands have meaningful relationships with their customers that go far beyond a single attribute.

Great brands are complex matrices of attributes, features, experiences, values, and emotions that bind the customer to them on a variety of levels. However, each strand of the brand is weak and easily broken by a competitive offer. That's why unidimensional brands are vulnerable. Look at each "connection" to the consumer as a single weak and fragile thread. Taken together, though, all of these threads can weave a strong fabric, binding the brand to the customer in a way that is all but unbreakable.

The great brands of today are diverse, yet consistent. Like a great actor who can take on many roles while maintaining the essence of who he or she is, a great brand is consistent, yet extendable; complex, yet universally understandable. A brand that does all of these things — a mega-brand — is the ultimate business weapon in today's world.

**Michael Capiraso
Principal,
Michael Capiraso
Consulting**

What makes a great brand? Whether it is a product or a service — whether it enhances, assists, or entertains — fundamentally, a brand must provide a connection. The quality of that connection and how deeply it impacts the consumer is the critical factor that catapults a brand to greatness. When we connect to a great brand, we have a visceral reaction. We feel an intrinsic, emotional link. We want to own it. We want to experience it again and again.

The source of this connection is linked to brand communication. At the NFL, Calvin Klein, and Cole Haan, I've worked with great brands that have great brand communication. Brand communication is the primary conduit through which consumers perceive the brand and the outlet in which they connect to it. Great experience, great product, great design, great advertising: these are the component pieces of brand communication that, when combined together cohesively, create the connection and make a great brand.

**Linda Kaplan Thaler
CEO, Chief
Creative Officer,
Kaplan Thaler Group**

In today's hypercompetitive, noisy marketplace, breaking through the clutter and getting your brand noticed is extremely challenging. Messages bombard us, no matter where we are, 24 hours a day, seven days a week. So how do you make a great brand in this age of information overload? Create a Bang!

A Bang! is a counterintuitive approach to commanding the spotlight and helps a brand explode into the marketplace virtually overnight. It creates a highly engaging, entertaining, and informative experience — one that establishes a strong connection between consumers and brands. A Bang! gets people talking across platforms and becomes part of the cultural dialogue. Its huge multiplier effect creates an ever-expanding universe for a brand, turning an occasional user into a fierce brand evangelical.

Aflac is a great example. Since the Aflac Duck first took flight, the brand catapulted from 11 percent to 95 percent household awareness, resulting in double-digit sales growth. Starbucks, Apple, and FedEx are other examples of great brands, because they forever altered the marketing landscape by creating a new way of thinking about a product or service.

**Michael Mohamad
Television
Consultant, Vidaroo
Inc.**

Great brands understand that brand building is a never-ending process. Some great brands — and there have been several over the last couple of years — have had some difficulties. Some management teams become stubborn when negative issues are brought to them. These issues can come from within or outside the company. Great brands confront negative issues quickly before they take on a life of their own. Brand building doesn't have to be complicated. In fact, you can build a world-class brand in three simple steps.

Step one is to work out who you are and what you stand for. All great brands clearly know what they stand for. And consumers are clear about what they can expect in return. That's what creates trust. And trust is the basic contract between the brand and the consumer.

Step two is to tell everyone in your organization who you are and what you stand for. Great brands know that everyone in the organization has to embrace the brand and deliver against the brand's principles and values.

Step three is to dance like no one's watching. To have fun. To try new things.

Branding doesn't have to be complicated. You just have to know who you are and have fun spreading the word.

James Gregory
Chief Executive Officer,
CoreBrand LLC

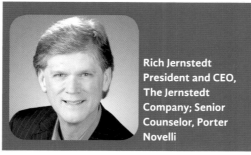

Rich Jernstedt
President and CEO,
The Jernstedt Company; Senior Counselor, Porter Novelli

The ultimate goal of business leadership is to efficiently build equity in the company. Yet the corporate brand, an asset that improves equity and increases efficiencies when managed properly, is often absent from the business leaders' agenda. Maybe it's because making the jump from a collection of words and colors to a truly great brand has always been viewed as something of a mystical endeavor, but there are tools available to help make this process easier and more accountable.

As a consumer, you look through this book and see a collection of great brands, but as a business decision maker you must see a collection of valuable assets that have been leveraged actively and consistently. By clarifying the role of the corporate brand, and explaining how the brand creates value in terms of both cash flow and stock performance, companies can transform their brand into a valuable financial asset.

The corporate brand is a company's most influential and valuable asset. It can help ensure that any company weakness or mistake has minimal and momentary reputational impact.

Great communications can create a "greatest brand." It ensures brand awareness, personality, distinctiveness. It can help generate understanding and relevance. In the best situations, it encourages engagement and other behaviors that achieve critical goals.

But even the best communications can't sustain a "greatest brand." This is an era of instant dissemination of information and opinion. Everything is local and global. And key stakeholders are smart, data-overwhelmed, and cynical. The company must have a strong, authentic corporate character, so that it doesn't just communicate like a great brand, it acts like one.

According to a new study by the Arthur W. Page Society, "In an age of unprecedented transparency, *how* we are is *who* we are."

Enjoy this edition. Learn from brands that act great because they are great.

Keith Reinhard
Chairman Emeritus,
DDB Worldwide

Kevin Roberts
Chief Executive Officer Worldwide,
Saatchi & Saatchi

Antony Young
President,
The Water Cooler Group

The 20th-century Spanish philosopher Jose Ortega y Gasset counseled, "The first act of any society is the selection of a point of view." And so it is for brands. A great brand is distinguished by a passionately held point of view, from which evolves a relevant and compelling promise — the combination of which is conveyed with a distinctive style and personality.

McDonald's point of view is that eating out is about more than food. It therefore attaches itself to contemporary lifestyles. Volkswagen's point of view is that automotive excellence should be available to everyone. It is therefore expanding its line in order to promise the unique Volkswagen driving experience to people of all economic classes . . . but always with the same special style that launched the Beetle in 1959.

A well-selected point of view, a compelling promise stated or implied, and a winning personality. These are the key elements of a great brand.

Brands are running out of juice. Even great brands are being squeezed hard by the erosion of premium pricing, the struggle to maintain differentiation, the rapid imitation of innovation, and ever more competition.

With consumers in control, the shifts are from market to movement, from inform to inspire, from distraction to interaction, from return on investment to return on involvement.

Brands that share priceless value will become Lovemarks. Quality, performance, and all the rest have become table-stakes. Only Lovemarks understand that long-term relationships are based on three human connectors: the thrill of mystery, the immediacy of sensuality, and the trust of intimacy.

Lovemarks are the future for America's great brands. Some have already made the leap to become super-evolved brands that make deep emotional connections with consumers . . . great brands that inspire loyalty beyond reason.

What is a great brand? A great brand is a badge that customers, employees, and shareholders want to wear. It should steer and shape a culture and aspiration of how a product or company should behave. Brands are what people buy into, not just buy. They spark the emotional and the irrational, and that's what helps to create a premium in perception and often in price. Finally, a great brand helps a company withstand bad news, awkward service, and lapses of judgment.

AECOM

Imagine it. Delivered.

THE MARKET

The pace of global change is faster than ever, and the opportunities and challenges being unearthed are as many as they are complex. Los Angeles–headquartered firm AECOM is tackling these issues head-on: from urbanization and climate change to next-generation infrastructure. Bringing together the infrastructure and real estate industries' most storied firms, AECOM has created a strong, integrated team of nearly 90,000 employees with the ability to design, build, finance, operate, and manage assets worldwide.

The company's coming of age has coincided with tumultuous times for clients as they face increasingly complex issues. The gulf between challenges faced and solutions required is one that AECOM is uniquely positioned to fill. The firm swiftly built a reputation for its ability to not just deliver in every sector, but to connect expertise across disciplines to create more innovative solutions — ensuring that whether it's iconic skyscrapers, restored environments, or modern transit systems, all of AECOM's projects benefit at their core from the firm's distinctive blend of experience and interconnected thinking.

ACHIEVEMENTS

Working in close partnerships with clients, AECOM's approach to challenging convention has earned recognition in the industry and beyond. In 2017 the company secured a place on *Fortune*'s list of the World's Most Admired Companies for the third consecutive year, while 2016 saw AECOM making the largest jump of the Fortune 500, catapulting from 343rd into the 156th position on the exclusive list.

Within the industry, AECOM continues to dominate rankings, securing *Engineering News*

Record's Top Design Firm ranking for the seventh consecutive year, as well as multiple number-one positions in construction, from general building to transportation and sports. AECOM's projects have also attracted illustrious recognition: the Sutong Bridge earned an American Society of Civil Engineers Outstanding Civil Engineering Achievement award; Msheireb, the Heart of Doha Masterplan won the World Architecture Future Project of the Year; and the American Public Works Association named the Hoover Dam one of the Projects of the Century.

HISTORY

Launched in 1990, AECOM merged five separate entities and built quickly on that foundation. Completing more than 50 mergers in the next 25 years, AECOM assembled an unparalleled stable of talent, carving out a distinctive position as the industry's most innovative solutions provider.

Firms joining the AECOM family included DMJM; consulting-engineering powerhouse Faber Maunsell; EDAW; architecture and engineering giant Ellerbe Becket; cost engineering and project management experts Davis Langdon; New York City construction giant Tishman; and during 2014 — a landmark year for the firm — URS and Hunt Construction Group. AECOM also expanded its capabilities to include financing with the creation in 2013 of its investment arm, AECOM Capital.

THE PRODUCT

Clients worldwide place their trust in AECOM to design, build, finance, and operate their most vital projects. Whether transforming concepts into assets, or creating reliable transportation networks or renewable energy sources, the firm has become renowned for its ability to cross-pollinate ideas across disciplines to come up with transformative solutions.

One of the firm's most recognizable projects was the rebuilding of the World Trade Center. The tallest building in the Western Hemisphere, One World Trade Center presented unique challenges due to its size, geographic constraints, and operational necessities. Providing preconstruction and construction management services, AECOM delivered the 104-story tower that has become a bold new icon for New York.

Another epic challenge was developing a transportable research facility for the British Antarctic Survey. Faced with some of Earth's harshest climates, Halley VI became the world's first fully relocatable, permanently manned Antarctic research station and received the 2015 American Society of Civil Engineers' Outstanding Civil Engineering Achievement Award.

AECOM has also played a crucial role in creating a more connected world. Just one example is the Sutong Bridge in China's Jiangsu province; the world's first cable-stayed bridge to surpass a 1,000-meter span, it provided vital transportation links in the region.

The firm has become a trusted partner of governments worldwide. Bringing expertise in design, construction, and operations, AECOM has managed some of the United States' largest nuclear decommissioning projects, including the Oak Ridge Reservation site in Tennessee.

RECENT DEVELOPMENTS

With creative thinking at its core, AECOM is leading many of the projects that are reshaping industries. With cities home to more than half of the world's population, AECOM is playing a key role in tackling urbanization's challenges. From masterplans and transport systems to ambitious resilience programs, AECOM's Cities group is working with urban centers worldwide to help

At the forefront of sustainable design and construction, AECOM works with clients worldwide to achieve ambitious environmental targets. As construction manager for the world's first LEED® Platinum skyscraper — One Bryant Park in New York City — AECOM delivered a 55-story tower that includes a five-megawatt cogeneration plant and an extensive gray water retention and recycling system. Another first, the firm also delivered the first indoor arena to achieve LEED® Platinum status: Sacramento's Golden 1 Center. One hundred percent of the arena's electricity comes from solar energy, allowing it to serve over 200 events annually at net-zero energy. Working with the US Navy's Space and Naval Warfare Systems Center Pacific (SPAWAR) facility to improve energy conservation across its 224 buildings, AECOM achieved a net energy reduction of 37 percent, reaching its goal two years ahead of schedule.

them adapt and thrive. In a first-of-its-kind venture, AECOM is a key partner in developing the smart city of Dholera, India. A benchmark for urban development, Dholera will run on clean energy and feature intelligent infrastructure, where a smart grid connects every home to utilities and digital services.

AECOM is also incubating the next generation of transportation technologies. Selected to design and build the first Hyperloop test track, AECOM is working to advance the development of Hyperloop Technologies' vision of transportation at speeds up to 800 miles per

hour. As autonomous vehicles become mainstream, the company is also preparing cities for the fundamental shift that transportation networks will need to undergo to facilitate this new technology.

Future-focused, AECOM is at the forefront of adopting new technologies, including next-generation BIM — building information modeling — which allows teams to create cloud-based, interactive 3D structure models to guide development and optimize use. The firm has also embraced immersive technologies such as virtual reality, becoming the first to use Microsoft VR HoloLens "mixed-reality" technology to allow users to experience projects in development.

PROMOTION

Celebrating the 10-year anniversary of its IPO in 2017, AECOM marked the occasion with the launch of a powerful brand identity. The firm's new tagline — "Imagine it. Delivered." — poses a compelling call to the marketplace, celebrating the firm's passion for working with visionary clients to bring the seemingly impossible to life. In 2017 AECOM also broke from industry norms by launching its first television commercial. With acclaimed director John Singleton at the helm, the commercial illustrates the enormous potential of infrastructure to change the way people live. The launch of the commercial formed part of a global integrated marketing campaign that aims to engage employees, clients, and stakeholders in considering the possibilities that the future can hold.

BRAND VALUES

To deliver a better world, AECOM champions six simple but powerful brand values.

- AECOM aims to **inspire** employees by celebrating their achievements and developing their skills, while working to elevate the communities the company serves.

- AECOM also champions the freedom to **dream** and reimagine what's possible.

- AECOM encourages its team to **collaborate** by building diverse teams that connect expertise to create innovative solutions.

- With a focus on solutions, AECOM highly values the ability to **anticipate** by understanding the complexity of clients' challenges and helping them see further.

- Closely connected is the commitment to **safeguard,** prioritizing safety, security, and ethical conduct.

- Last but not least, great ideas are nothing without the ability to **deliver.** AECOM is focused on delivering operational excellence and flawless execution on every project, big or small.

THINGS YOU DIDN'T KNOW ABOUT AECOM

- ○ AECOM built more than half of all professional sports stadiums between 2006 and 2016, and has designed more NBA arenas than any other firm.

- ○ AECOM helped create Spaceport America — Gateway to Space, the world's first commercial spaceport, in New Mexico.

- ○ AECOM has helped the US government safely destroy more than 90 percent of its chemical weapons stockpile.

THE MARKET

Food and drink are at the heart of family gatherings, holiday celebrations, and connections with friends. From Super Bowl festivities to summer picnics and Thanksgiving meals, it's easy to overindulge from time to time. Whether it's a holiday or weekday, individuals enjoy seeking out good times with friends and family.

While food and drink help people connect, overindulgence can lead to heartburn, acid indigestion, upset stomach, and headaches. For 85 years, Alka-Seltzer® has been providing fast relief to millions of consumers with its unique formula designed to alleviate both stomach and head pain.

ACHIEVEMENTS

Alka-Seltzer is one of the most iconic brands in American history, generating great nostalgic imagery that has kept the brand a mainstay of popular culture for 85 years. In fact, Alka-Seltzer has long been associated with some of the most memorable and oft-quoted ads in U.S. television history.

Rooted in American popular culture, the brand is well-known for its historical creative and memorable advertising campaigns, including "Speedy Alka-Seltzer" and the famous jingle "Plop, Plop, Fizz, Fizz, Oh What A Relief It Is®." Other famous, award-winning campaigns include 1969's "Mama Mia, That's a Spicy

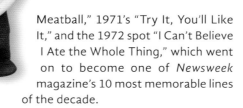

Meatball," 1971's "Try It, You'll Like It," and the 1972 spot "I Can't Believe I Ate the Whole Thing," which went on to become one of *Newsweek* magazine's 10 most memorable lines of the decade.

HISTORY

Launched in 1931 Alka-Seltzer remains one of the most well-known over-the-counter products in the United States. Alka-Seltzer was introduced by Miles Laboratories and brought to market as a remedy for headaches and indigestion.

Known as a popular brand with a rich history, the effervescent Alka-Seltzer tablet gently breaks up and dissolves the full feeling of indigestion, heartburn, and pain.

In 1951 the famous baby-faced character Speedy Alka-Seltzer was born, featuring an Alka-Seltzer tablet body with hat and "effervescent" wand. Originally known as Sparky, his name was changed by a sales manager to reflect that year's promotional theme, "Speedy Relief." In 1964 the original six-inch-high doll was insured for $100,000 and kept in the vault of a Beverly Hills bank.

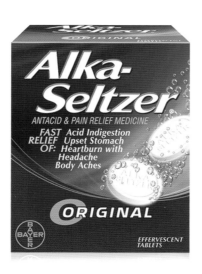

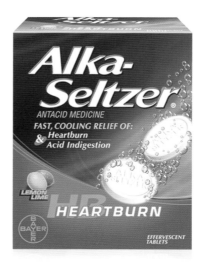
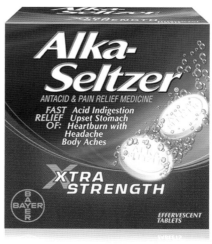

THE PRODUCT

Alka-Seltzer's unique formula is a combination of aspirin (acetylsalicylic acid), citric acid, and sodium bicarbonate. The product is available in the form of two effervescent tablets (one inch in diameter) which actively dissolve in a four-ounce glass of water. Once dissolved, the acid and bicarbonate react, producing carbon dioxide gas (also known as the "seltzer" in Alka-Seltzer). The word "alka" is derived from alkali.

People ask all the time, "What is effervescence?" They've heard that term associated with Alka-Seltzer for years and years. Is it the bubbles? What makes the bubbles? And why do those effervescent bubbles work?

Yes, it's the bubbles! They're the result of a series of chemical interactions that provide speedy relief, fast. "Effervescence" refers to the unique and lively bubbling form that creates "The Alka-Seltzer® Experience." After dropping the tablets into water, you can be assured that relief is on the way. Simply put, the medicine dissolves fast and is ready to go to work the instant you take it. The time it would take for a pill to dissolve is eliminated.

Alka-Seltzer is now available in a wide variety of formulas and flavors, including Original, great-tasting Lemon-Lime, Xtra Strength for the most powerful relief, Alka-Seltzer Heartburn, and Alka-Seltzer Gold. For those people who prefer chewable heartburn relief, consumers can take Alka-Seltzer Gummies — fruit-flavored, soft, and easy to chew. Extra-strength ReliefChew tablets offer relief from heartburn and are designed for the on-the-go customer.

The product continues to be a tried-and-true remedy for heartburn, acid indigestion, and upset stomach with headache and body pains. Word of its effectiveness is found not only on drugstore and pharmacy shelves, but also throughout the TV airwaves via creative and memorable advertising campaigns as well as on the Internet.

RECENT DEVELOPMENTS

Launch of the Alka-Seltzer chewable varieties in May 2013 resulted in the brand's resurgence in the antacid tablet business. Brand sales rose an astonishing 580.5 percent after their introduction. The brand's gummy-like formula is appealing to a new consumer generation, as well as older consumers who don't like pills.

PROMOTION

Eight Alka-Seltzer commercials have won Clio awards,

BIG LEAGUE RELIEF.

SPEEDY

AFTER THE CHILI DOGS, NACHOS AND LUKEWARM BEER, ONLY ALKA-SELTZER HAS WHAT IT TAKES TO SETTLE BOTH YOUR STOMACH AND YOUR HEAD. NOW THAT'S THE PERFECT DOUBLE-PLAY.

PLOP, PLOP, FIZZ, FIZZ. OH WHAT A RELIEF IT IS!

BAYER

USE AS DIRECTED.   ALKASELTZER.COM

©2010 BAYER HEALTHCARE LLC

the ad industry's equivalent of the Oscars. The remedy's first spokesman was the animated, stop-action sprite from the early fifties, Speedy Alka-Seltzer. Radio actor Dick Beals served as the voice of Speedy in more than 100 commercials. Speedy Alka-Seltzer reigned for more than 10 years, and in the seventies again graced TV screens, singing the new "Plop, Plop, Fizz, Fizz" jingle, which ran from 1975 to 1980. Speedy appeared with Buster Keaton, blasted off in a rocket to the moon, and sang and danced with Sammy Davis Jr. In 2009 Speedy resurfaced in an Alka-Seltzer Plus commercial with Olympic skier Lindsey Vonn, appearing on her skis to give her a competitive advantage.

The Alka-Seltzer brand's best-loved television spots have traditionally focused on fictional sufferers like "Jack," the star of the "Mama Mia, That's a Spicy Meatball," an award-winning 1970 campaign. In 1971's "Try It, You'll Like It," the protagonist samples an unusual dish recommended by his waiter — with disastrous results. Even though "Ralph" couldn't believe he "ate the whole thing" in 1972, that line went on to become one of *Newsweek* magazine's 10 most memorable lines of the decade. In 2005 a remake of "I Can't Believe" was launched in honor of the brand's 75th anniversary in 2006. The ad was a playful salute featuring Doris Roberts and Peter Boyle of *Everybody Loves Raymond* fame. In each of these historical ads, the fictional sufferers have experienced upset stomach and pain from overindulgence, and Alka-Seltzer has been the remedy providing relief to them all.

SPEEDY

ALKA SELTZER

BRAND VALUES

Alka-Seltzer is a brand that people associate with relief from overindulgence in food and drink. The values most associated with the Alka-Seltzer brand are as follows:

- **Effective.** For 85 years, consumers have been relying on Alka-Seltzer for its effective relief. In return, Alka-Seltzer has been committed to providing the highest-quality relief to its consumers.

- **Multisymptom.** Consumers use Alka-Seltzer products not only to treat their upset stomachs but to combat their headaches and body aches. Alka-Seltzer is different from other antacid brands as it is the only leading brand that provides this dual stomach and pain benefit to consumers.

- **Reliable.** Alka-Seltzer has a long heritage and has been trusted for 85 years. Alka-Seltzer's products are a staple in many households.

- **Spirited.** Over the years, Alka-Seltzer has leveraged its heritage in humorous advertising to connect with its consumer.

THINGS YOU DIDN'T KNOW ABOUT ALKA-SELTZER

○ To test out a new camera, NASA astronauts in 2015 dripped blue and red food dye into a floating globule of water and then inserted an Alka-Seltzer tablet into it. The mixture began effervescing *from the inside out*, with the tablet jumping around inside the mixture.

○ The search for Speedy's voice resulted in more than 400 auditions. Twenty-four-year-old radio actor Dick Beals landed the role, and Speedy's voice was created. Speedy appeared in 212 commercials from 1954 to 1964. The original Speedy doll was lost en route to the Philippines in 1971, but was found in an Australian warehouse five years later.

○ Father of actress Julianna Margulies (of TV show *ER* fame), Paul Margulies, wrote the "Plop, Plop, Fizz, Fizz, Oh What a Relief It Is" theme song.

○ Kim Basinger, Morgan Freeman, and Sammy Davis Jr. are among the celebrities who have appeared in Alka-Seltzer commercials.

○ Alka-Seltzer used to be sold in glass tubes, which were discontinued in 1984 to reduce costs and eliminate breakage problems.

CORPORATION
Andersen®

HISTORY

Danish immigrant Hans Andersen and his family began Andersen as a lumberyard in 1903. The Andersen family opened for business along the St. Croix River in Hudson, Wisconsin. From this location, they used the river to transport logs directly to the site. Andersen soon specialized in window frames, selling more than 100,000 in 1909 alone. In 1913 Andersen moved across the river to Bayport, Minnesota, where its headquarters and main manufacturing facility remain to this day.

Today Andersen employs more than 9,000 people, with manufacturing facilities across North America.

ACHIEVEMENTS

From the start, three underlying principles have motivated every Andersen innovation: energy efficiency, beauty, and durability.

At the turn of the 20th century, window frames and sash were commonly made on-site during construction. Standardizing sizes and manufacturing in a controlled environment were the logical next steps toward improved quality and performance. In 1905, such standardization proved to be the first innovation of founder Hans Andersen when he invented the "two-bundle" method of making window frames. Horizontal and vertical frame parts in incremental sizes were bundled separately, and they could be assembled into a window frame in just 10 minutes. As a result, builders could more efficiently create windows in sizes people wanted and dealers could stock the parts at a lower cost.

By 1932 Andersen eliminated the need for on-site assembly altogether with the industry's first fully manufactured window unit, the Andersen® master casement.

Andersen's 1966 invention of Perma-Shield® exterior cladding all but guaranteed peace of

mind for homeowners. Perma-Shield cladding protects the exterior and virtually eliminates maintenance.

From the 1970s to the 1990s Andersen continued to set the pace for innovation with advancements in energy-efficient design and Low-E glass technology.

In 1991 Andersen developed the revolutionary Fibrex® material — a composite made of vinyl and wood fiber reclaimed from Andersen manufacturing. Fibrex material exhibits some of the best thermal and low-maintenance qualities of both its source materials. Strong and water resistant, Andersen uses Fibrex material across its product lines.

Andersen products have come a long way since the two-bundle system of 1905. Yet the vision remains: "To lead the window and door industry by creating products and services that are different and better as measured by our customers."

Andersen windows and doors are now available in nearly unlimited sizes, shapes, styles, and price points.

As Andersen continues to refine and develop products, the focus remains on applying the right material for the right application. This approach allows Andersen to develop highly innovative product lines boasting practicality, efficiency, and design flexibility. Also, Andersen windows and doors are all covered by Andersen's exclusive Owner-to-Owner® limited warranty. While most other window warranties end

when a home is sold, Andersen's coverage — 20 years on glass, 10 years on nonglass parts — is completely transferable from each owner to the next.

In response to a rapidly changing marketplace, Andersen now offers an expanded portfolio that complements a diverse range of building, remodeling, and replacement projects. The expansion has allowed the brand to compete strongly where it has never competed before, offering replacement, remodeling, and new construction solutions for virtually any style home, including single-family living, multifamily housing, and light commercial construction.

LEGACY

Andersen's longstanding practice of making products that perform for generations allows the company to offer some of the industry's best warranties. The company still offers parts for windows and doors built long ago.

And it isn't just history that makes Andersen an industry leader but rather a commitment to innovation. Andersen always sets new standards for windows and doors that raise the bar for the entire industry. Being around since 1903 means Andersen hasn't just seen where the industry's been. Andersen guides where it's going.

Andersen and Habitat for Humanity have partnered for more than 20 years to build quality affordable homes for families across the country, and around the world. Andersen is partnering with St. Croix Valley Habitat to build 18 net-zero, energy-efficient homes in River Falls, Wisconsin. In addition, Andersen donated funds to Twin Cities Habitat to assist with building their new headquarters in St. Paul, Minnesota. The building proudly features Andersen 100 Series Windows.

In 2007 Andersen completed its 100 Years 100 Homes project in partnership with Habitat for Humanity. Launched in 2003 to commemorate the company's 100-year milestone, Andersen committed to funding and building 100 Habitat homes.

LOOKING AHEAD

Everyone has a different idea of "home," and the dream of owning a home remains alive and well. For over a century, Andersen Corporation has focused on turning ideas into reality. With brands including Andersen, American Craftsman, Renewal by Andersen, Silver Line, and Weiland, Andersen windows and doors make it easier to dream about home — easier to design and easier to install.

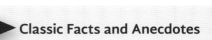

Classic Facts and Anecdotes

- Andersen has been on the leading edge of mass production and customization technologies since it first began mass production in 1904 — a full nine years before Henry Ford put the automobile on an assembly line.

- In 1914 Andersen Corporation created one of the first employee profit-sharing programs. This vision continues today in a progressive attitude of sharing the rewards of success with employees, as demonstrated through substantial employee ownership of the company.

- In 1923 Andersen became the first in the industry to offer two weeks paid vacation to all 295 employees — a novelty in the woodworking industry at the time.

- In 2012 the Andersen Corporate Foundation celebrated 70 years of giving. This foundation makes donations to hundreds of nonprofit organizations annually, providing affordable housing, activities, and awareness in health, safety, education, youth development, and civic and human services in the communities where Andersen employees live and work. To date, the foundation has donated more than $50 million across North America in the communities Andersen employees call home.

GREEN FOCUS

From the beginning, Andersen has built a reputation for environmental stewardship and producing energy-efficient products. Among the many distinctions the company has received, Andersen was among the first window companies in the nation to meet ENERGY STAR performance requirements in all geographic regions. The company was also the first window manufacturer accepted into the Environmental Protection Agency's ENERGY STAR program and was awarded the 2016 ENERGY STAR Partner of the Year distinction for its family of brands. Andersen published its first corporate sustainability report in 2012.

As a company devoted to environmental stewardship, Andersen strives to minimize pollution, conserve natural resources, promote energy conservation, develop long-lasting products, and continuously improve the organization's environmental performance overall. People who select Andersen windows and doors are choosing products that are energy efficient, sustainable, and durable.

HISTORY

Annin Flagmakers is a 168-year-old corporation headquartered in New Jersey. The American flag was scarcely 70 years old in 1847 when brothers Benjamin and Edward Annin founded Annin & Co. on Fulton Street in New York City. The business had begun with their father, Alexander Annin, who had been sewing flags and supplying them to merchant ships from his sailmaking shop on the New York City waterfront as far back as 1820. There, the company prospered and grew along with the nation. Annin & Co. incorporated in 1910. It now operates as three separate companies: Annin Flagmakers, FlagZone LLC, and Starfields LLC. Annin Flagmakers has over 500 employees, with factories in South Boston, Virginia, and Coshocton, Ohio. FlagZone has 200 employees and is located in Gilbertsville, Pennsylvania. Starfields has 50 employees and operates out of Cobbs Creek, Virginia.

In 1865 Annin experienced its first big surge in business when the Civil War ignited the fires of patriotism in the American populace. For the first time in America's history, private citizens purchased American flags in significant numbers to display on their homes. Increased demand for American flags coincided with the nation's industrial revolution in the latter part of the 19th century. Annin Flagmakers, always on the forefront of technology, made the motorized sewing machine a standard piece of flag-making equipment.

Demand for U.S. flags boomed again in 1917 with entry into World War I. Annin's new flagship plant in Verona, New Jersey, was fully modernized for its time, with all of the latest equipment and a dedicated and skilled workforce. Brand-new machines, such as mechanized die-cutters for stamping out stars, were invented specifically to automate the flag-making process and were installed at the Verona plant. Assembly lines, popularized by Henry Ford, were also set up to increase efficiencies. The management of Annin Flagmakers made certain that the methods of production in their factories kept pace with 20th-century progress.

Historically, the domestic political climate and world events have affected U.S. flag sales in a way that is unique compared with other products. While sales of American flags dipped during the Depression years, they rose again during the patriotic fervor of World War II. The addition of the new states of Alaska in 1959 and Hawaii in 1960 generated an avalanche of orders from Americans who wanted to replace their outdated 48-star U.S. flags with the new 50-star version. Anti–Vietnam War sentiment during the turbulent period of the late sixties and early seventies made those years lean ones for U.S. flag sales, but America's bicentennial in 1976 brought Old Glory back stronger than ever. The patriotic fervor that gripped the people of the United States after the tragic events of September 11, 2001, led to an unprecedented demand for American flags. Orders poured in for quantities of U.S. flags that were twenty times that of normal. Annin Flagmakers rose to the occasion and dramatically increased production.

In 2005, Annin Flagmakers joined with other domestic flag manufacturing companies as a founding member of the Flag Manufacturers Association of America (FMAA), dedicated to promoting the manufacture of U.S. flags in America by Americans with domestically made fabric. Annin continuously looks for ways to provide better service to its customers in an omni-channel environment by blending experienced staff with technology to offer a secure portal order management system, an e-Commerce Dealer website program, and Electronic Data Interchange (EDI) capabilities. Annin prides itself on the quality of its products and the experience of its people, many of whom have more than 20 and 30 years of experience with the company.

Evolution of the Annin Flagmakers Logo

Mid-1800s	Late 1800s	1800s ~ 1900s	1956	1960s	1968

ACHIEVEMENTS

Annin Flagmakers designs flags for how and where they are flown, incorporating technological advancements into its manufacturing processes. Inside Annin's Virginia and Ohio factories, U.S. flags are manufactured with advanced stand-up sewing production techniques. State, international, and custom flags are digitally printed and screen-dyed to exact color specifications. Annin's in-house research and testing laboratories, together with its art department, are constantly monitoring dye formulas. The brand's distribution systems are in real-time compliance with customer requirements.

Annin has created its own inks with UV inhibitors to create bright, colorfast products that withstand the elements of weather, wind, and sun. Annin Flagmakers owns several trademarks on its materials with the most popular being Tough-Tex, Nyl-Glo, Bulldog, and Signature. Today the company sells more than 10 million flags nationwide to business and residential consumers.

Cultivating its brand identity and brand promise over 168 years, and as a B2B company, consumers, businesses, and the media recognize Annin as the brand in flags. Over the years, Annin Flagmakers has been featured in the media to educate the public on American-made products and how a flag is made. Annin has appeared in such programs as ABC World News Tonight's *Made in America* series, the History Channel's *Modern Marvels,* the Science Channel's *How Do They Do It?,* National Geographic's *July 4th: Exploding the Myths,* and John Ratzenberger's *American Made.*

Annin flags have flown over the White House and on foreign fields of battle—at the Argonne Offensive and the Battle of Guadalcanal. From the top of Mount Suribachi on Iwo Jima to the surface of the moon, Annin flags have been there to represent core American ideals. Annin Flagmakers has established its brand identity and leadership throughout history, with other prominent roles in world events including:

- The inauguration of Abraham Lincoln and the flag that draped his casket as it was taken by train from Washington, DC, to Illinois.

- The opening ceremonies of the Brooklyn Bridge in 1883.

- Commander Robert E. Peary's arrival at the North Pole in 1909 and Rear Admiral

Richard E. Byrd's arrival at the South Pole 21 years later.

- The design and inception of the POW-MIA flag in 1979 in conjunction with the National League of Families of POW/MIA.

- The 10th anniversary of September 11, 2011, with the Flag of Honor / Flag of Heroes project displaying a Remembrance Field of Honor in Battery Park, New York, with 3,000 Flags of Honor and the flags of 93 nations representing all who lost their lives at all locations on 9/11.

LEGACY

Annin Flagmakers, a family-owned business since 1847, is still owned by the Beard and Dennis families, fifth-generation direct descendants of Alexander Annin. The company is run today by sixth-generation family members Carter Beard, president, and Sandy Dennis Van Lieu, executive vice president. The 2015 senior management team includes Ken Baum, executive vice president and CFO; Mary Repke, senior vice president of sales and marketing; Richard Caramagna, vice president of operations; and Bob Caggiano, vice president of commercial sales.

Technology has also played a role in how the company chooses to work in order to cultivate the most talented and empowered employees. In 2012, Annin Flagmakers implemented a ROWE (Results-Oriented Workplace Environment) philosophy to reflect its ability to respond to the everyday demands and challenges of today's worker. As such, Annin employees focus on

deliverables and measured results without the traditional requirement of having to be physically present in a business office setting.

The company and its employees are passionate about the fact that they make the U.S. flag. The company decided that it was most important to recognize veterans and their families for the sacrifices they make on the nation's behalf. As such, Annin is a goodwill ambassador honoring veterans' organizations and supporting specific historical events and programs sponsored by leading civic and military organizations and veteran-based charities.

LOOKING AHEAD

Annin Flagmakers stays true to its vision to be the world's premier manufacturer and distributor of flag products. The company continually strives to be the industry leader by servicing all of its markets with high-quality products, fair prices, and the best service in the industry. By conducting its business with the highest level of integrity, Annin achieves growth through innovative programs, new product offerings, and maximizing efficiencies through state-of-the-art operations.

▶ Classic Facts and Anecdotes

- In 1947, *New York Mirror* magazine covered the erection of what was then the largest free-flying U.S. flag (90 by 60 feet). Annin's client was the Port Authority of New York and New Jersey, which operates the George Washington Bridge. The flag was made of Nylanin, a tough nylon-wool blend codeveloped by Annin.

- The aftermath of 9/11 brought about many poignant moments. A civil servant from New York City called Annin to buy casket-sized flags with which to drape the remains of the victims at Ground Zero.

- The U.S. Olympic Committee partnered with Annin for its Raise Our Flag fundraising campaign for the 2012 Summer Olympics, which raised $351,084 from 29,257 donated stitches. USOC supporters donated money to buy stitches in a virtual flag, visible in the virtual world as it took shape online.

1981	1991	Present Day

ARROW
USA · 1851

HISTORY

In the 1820s, from her home in Troy, New York, Mrs. Hannah Montague created the first detachable shirt collar. As the popularity of the detachable collar increased over the course of the first half of the 19th century, many companies in Troy began manufacturing and selling collars as well. In 1885, one such company adopted the ARROW trademark in connection with its products. This company went through a series of mergers and name changes, eventually becoming known as Cluett, Peabody & Co. in the late 1890s.

In 1905 Cluett, Peabody & Co. began an advertising campaign that featured a stylish young man wearing an ARROW shirt. This character later became known as the "Arrow Collar Man." The advertisements were illustrated by J. C. Leyendecker, a well-known commercial artist who also created cover art for the *Saturday Evening Post*. The campaign was a huge success. The fictional "Arrow Collar Man" character became an American icon, receiving more than 17,000 fan letters a day at the height of his popularity. The "Arrow Collar Man" inspired the Broadway musical *Helen of Troy, New York* in 1923, and President Theodore Roosevelt is noted to have referred to him as a "superb portrait" of the "common man."

The "Arrow Collar Man" generated so much demand for ARROW detachable collars that Cluett, Peabody & Co. expanded its line in 1918 to include approximately 400 different styles. However, during World War I, soldiers became accustomed to their collared uniform shirts, thus causing the detachable collar to lose popularity by the late 1920s.

In response to an increased demand for attached collars, ARROW introduced the "Trump" shirt in the late 1920s, and within several years had introduced collared dress shirts in colors and stripes. At this time, Cluett, Peabody & Co. became known for its "Sanforized" shirts — shirts that were treated with a patented process to relax the yarns in the fabric and prevent the shirt from shrinking.

Throughout the years, ARROW has continued to respond to shifting fashion trends. As the white-shirted stability of the 1950s gave way to the turbulent 1960s, the ARROW collection was grown to include more colorful designs. By 1968, fewer than half of the ARROW shirts sold were solid white. The ARROW line was redesigned in the 1970s with synthetic fabrics, tapering darts, and oversized collars inspired by the disco era, and again in the 1980s to adjust to the resurgence of classic tailoring that appealed to the conservatism of the young urban professional.

1851	1885	1905	1920	1923	1934
A small collar company begins manufacturing collars, eventually becoming Cluett, Peabody & Co.	The ARROW trademark is first used to promote collars and cuffs	J. C. Leyendecker, a commercial artist hired by Cluett, Peabody & Co., creates the famous "ARROW Collar Man"	Business is booming, and the company's line of collars expands to over 400 different styles	The "ARROW Collar Man" is the inspiration behind the Broadway musical, *Helen of Troy, New York*	ARROW collars become a staple in American culture; Cole Porter references them in his song, "You're the Top," which includes the line, "You're the top, You're an Arrow Collar"

The dress shirt market rebounded after a downswing in the 1990s, which saw the ARROW brand transferred through a series of owners and bankruptcies, as the millennium brought renewed interest to this market segment. PVH Corp. acquired the worldwide rights to the ARROW brand in 2004, revitalizing the brand and leading to many new and pivotal partnerships and campaigns. ARROW has gained much popularity since its humble beginning and continues to be regarded as a leader in American men's fashion.

ACHIEVEMENTS

ARROW commands extraordinary brand recognition for fashionable yet functional apparel. As one of the top-selling men's woven sport shirts in U.S. department and chain stores, ARROW shirts are known for quality, American style and sophistication, and innovation. The ARROW brand was featured in the Ivy Style exhibition at The Museum at FIT — Fashion Institute of Technology — and the associated publication *Ivy Style*.

LEGACY

One of the biggest problems with clothing up to the early 20th century was shrinkage. Clothes would continue to shrink after repeated washings, particularly collars and cuffs. In the 1920s, as soft-collar shirts were rising in popularity, Sanford Cluett, a nephew of the company's founders, began working on a process that would virtually "preshrink" fabric — a process called Controlled Compressive Shrinking. By 1930 the process was officially registered with the "Sanforized" trademark, and the company ceased all collar manufacturing in favor of "Sanforized" shirts. Soon the process was being licensed to other manufacturers, and today, later generations of sanforizing are still being used worldwide for cotton-based fabrics.

Offerings under the ARROW brand include a broad assortment of apparel, including dress shirts, neckwear, sportswear, and accessories. ARROW sportswear is about classic styling that is desirable and understandable by today's "Arrow Collar Man." The ARROW line consists of comfortable fabrics and styling and is intended to be wearable clothing for casual workdays that are transitional into weekend wear. ARROW sportswear is also durable and easy to care for. PVH is committed to providing quality apparel products throughout the world that embody the heritage of the ARROW brand and deliver superior quality to consumers.

LOOKING AHEAD

PVH will continue to manufacture quality ARROW products that are fashionable and affordable. The brand's look and appeal reflect a youthfulness and optimism that embody the American spirit. The ARROW brand represents conviction, dedication, and accomplishment, and as a result, ARROW remains at the forefront of the men's apparel industry.

Classic Facts and Anecdotes

- PVH maintains an extensive archive of ARROW merchandise, including collars, bow ties, shirt patterns, and advertising, such as magazine advertisements, dating back to as early as 1870.

- Cluett created ARROW collars of unique sizes for the famous 3.35-foot-tall Tom Thumb (11"-by-1" collar) and a giant Russian man (27.5"-by-5" collar), which was one of the largest collars ever produced for actual wear.

PVH

1941   **1963**   **1976**   **1995**   **2004**   **2012**

1941	1963	1976	1995	2004	2012
ARROW advertises the largest collar produced to date for Russian giant, measuring 27.5"x5"	In order to promote the ARROW Tournament Collection "Golf Line," the brand sponsors the 1963 Masters Tournament	Joe Namath teams up with the ARROW brand to promote the Joe Namath product line	Fabio promotes the ARROW At Work / At Play campaign	PVH Corp. acquires Cluett, Peabody & Co.	A 1920s ARROW collar ad by J. C. Leyendecker appears in the remake of *The Great Gatsby*

AXA EQUITABLE
redefining / standards

HISTORY

Although AXA is a global company, it operates through national affiliates, each bringing its own tradition into the AXA family. A prime example is AXA Equitable Life Insurance Company in the United States, with its rich history of strength and innovation.

Founder Henry Baldwin Hyde took a job with Mutual Life Insurance Company of New York, then America's largest insurer, in 1853. At Mutual, Hyde saw the best and thought he could do better. In spring 1859 he opened an office upstairs from Mutual and hung a banner announcing the arrival of the Equitable Life Assurance Society of the United States.

Hyde began a tradition of product innovation by adapting the tontine, a type of annuity dating back 200 years. In 1868 Equitable introduced four tontine policies that paid guaranteed death benefits and dividends. Between 1869 and 1899 the company's assets grew from $10.5 million to $280 million, making Equitable one of the largest and most powerful financial institutions in the world.

Equitable introduced in 1911 the first modern group life insurance policy. During World War I, Equitable paid death benefits on soldiers killed in battle. After World War II, Equitable was the biggest private lender of farm and residential loans. Its mortgages were tied to whole life policies, which guaranteed the loans and built up funds to pay off the mortgages.

In 1968 Equitable was the first New York company approved to market variable annuities, and in 1976 it pioneered variable life insurance. The company was the first to gain New York State approval for universal life insurance in 1983, and two years later introduced Incentive Life®, a hybrid of universal and variable life products. That same year Equitable became a full-service financial protection company with its acquisition of investment firm Donaldson, Lufkin and Jenrette (DLJ) and money manager Alliance Capital Management L.P.

French-based AXA Group* acquired Equitable in 1991 and changed its name to AXA Equitable in 1999. On July 8, 2004, the circle was closed when the MONY Group, the company that founder Henry Hyde left to create the Equitable, became a wholly owned subsidiary of AXA Financial.

ACHIEVEMENTS

Today AXA is truly an international company, operating in 59 countries, serving more than 103 million individual and corporate clients, and employing 166,000 people worldwide — impressive numbers for a company that just turned 30 years old. In 1985 a group of three French insurance companies adopted the name AXA. Within 10 years AXA became the largest French insurer and grew throughout Europe and beyond, into the United States in 1991 and Australia in 1995.

AXA's development has continued apace. In the financial crisis of 2007–2008 — the most severe in recent decades — AXA demonstrated its capacity to deliver results by remaining

focused on its core business: insurance and asset management. AXA's commitment is to stand by its clients with financial protection and savings solutions.

AXA Equitable offers a complete product portfolio of life insurance, annuities, and investments. Carrying on its tradition of innovation, AXA Equitable continues to develop products that provide real protection strategies. In 2010, for example, AXA Equitable introduced Retirement Cornerstone℠, a variable deferred annuity that has several ways to generate guaranteed lifetime income. *Guarantees are based*

launched an iPhone app for women, and a special section of the company's website focuses on the AXA Equitable Connection. In addition, AXA Equitable has partnered with the Global Fund for Women, an organization that helps make grants to women's groups that work to gain freedom from poverty, violence, and discrimination.

LOOKING AHEAD

AXA's business is financial protection. At a time when traditional solutions for retirement, such as defined benefit plans and Social Security, cannot be relied on; when baby boomers worry about outliving their assets; when the array of investment and saving options from which to choose can be dizzying, people want and need advice to help them make choices and plan for their future. They want and need innovative financial products from a company they can trust. Today, 103 million clients worldwide look to AXA for financial protection. They trust AXA's financial professionals to deliver guidance and to provide a full range of products to help meet their insurance, savings, and retirement needs and to help them develop the long-term plans that are essential to attaining financial independence in the 21st century.

AXA Equitable's strategy for the United States is designed to build on the history and name recognition of the Equitable Life Assurance Society of the United States while partnering the brand and positioning it globally with AXA.

*"AXA Group" refers to AXA, a French holding company for a group of international insurance and financial services companies, together with its direct and indirect consolidated subsidies.

on the claims-paying ability of the issuing insurance company.

Wherever clients are in their lives — starting a family or starting a business, newly wed or newly retired — AXA Equitable's highly trained professionals work with clients to tailor

financial strategies with the products and services needed to help them live, grow, and succeed.

LEGACY

AXA Equitable's commitment to its customers is reflected in the brand's values: To be attentive, reliable, and available. The company's goal is to make each interaction positive — from clients' calls to the service center to their experiences with the company's financial professionals. Working with AXA Equitable is not about buying a policy; it's about developing a relationship with an experienced, attentive financial pro.

AXA Equitable is dedicated to education as well — for clients as well as students. The AXA Foundation is the philanthropic arm of AXA Equitable, directing the company's philanthropic and volunteer activities and working to improve the quality of life in communities across the country where AXA has a presence.

The AXA Foundation's signature program, *AXA Achievement*, provides two resources that help make college possible: access and advice.

AXA Equitable is also committed to the women's market and launched the AXA Equitable Connection: *Women, Wealth and Wisdom* — an education and empowerment program. One of the program's primary goals is to connect women consumers to the education, resources, and guidance necessary to take control of their finances. Another goal is to foster volunteer efforts to help in partnership with outside organizations, such as Dress for Success. The AXA Equitable Connection seeks to build, for women employees and financial professionals, a community that enhances workplace opportunities for growth and development. To support this initiative, the company

Classic Facts and Anecdotes

- In 1881 Equitable pioneered the practice of paying death claims immediately and without protest — a departure from the industry's typical waiting period. This step reassured beneficiaries that poverty would be averted without delay.

- Equitable in the 1920s became the first company to deliver a claim check by air. The claim was processed in the home office, and a check delivered to the West Coast within three days.

- AXA Equitable's famous policyholders include eight presidents, Babe Ruth, George Burns, J. D. Rockefeller, Walter Chrysler, and W. K. Kellogg.

- AXA Financial's headquarters, 1290 Avenue of the Americas in Manhattan, is home to the world-famous mural *America Today,* by Thomas Hart Benton. Equitable purchased the 10-panel masterpiece in 1981. The mural graces the entrance to "1290," where building tenants, art lovers, and tourists alike can see it.

- French insurance companies are required to invest assets in agriculture. AXA chose to invest in grape growing. AXA Millesimes owns châteaus in Bordeaux and Languedoc, France, as well as vineyards in Portugal and Hungary.

- A number of airlines borrowed money from Equitable after World War II. Equitable played a significant role in the exploits of "the Aviator" himself by lending Howard Hughes $40 million in 1945 for Trans World Airlines. The much-needed loan is mentioned in the 2004 biopic about Hughes.

THE MARKET

Baskin-Robbins has always been about "More flavors . . . and more fun." Over the course of its 70-plus-year history, Baskin-Robbins has created more than 1,200 ice cream flavors to delight its guests, all served in fun, welcoming shops around the world. Ice cream lovers of all ages visit Baskin-Robbins shops to enjoy their favorite ice cream flavors and frozen desserts served any way they like. Whether they're purchasing an ice cream cake for an upcoming celebration, a cone to celebrate a Little League victory, or a sundae for a "just because" treat, over 300 million happy guests visit Baskin-Robbins restaurants each year.

Baskin-Robbins is an iconic ice cream brand that offers high-quality ice cream, specialty frozen desserts, and frozen beverages to its customers around the globe. Despite being the world's largest chain of ice cream specialty shops, Baskin-Robbins upholds a fun, neighborhood ice cream parlor feel that adds to the experience of enjoying its great-tasting ice cream. Baskin-Robbins strongly believes in the social aspect of ice cream, and has designed its shops as gathering spots for people who want to indulge, celebrate, and be refreshed. Irv Robbins, a cofounder of Baskin-Robbins, once summed up the company's community and happiness-focused philosophy by saying, "We sell fun, not ice cream."

ACHIEVEMENTS

Baskin-Robbins has emerged as a beloved meeting place for ice cream enthusiasts around the globe. Guests feel strong, long-term connections to the brand, leading many people to refer affectionately to their local shop as "my Baskin-Robbins."

Named the top ice cream and frozen dessert franchise in the United States by *Entrepreneur* magazine's 37th annual Franchise 500 ranking in 2016, Baskin-Robbins is the world's largest chain of ice cream specialty shops. Baskin-Robbins creates and markets innovative, premium ice cream, as well as specialty frozen desserts and beverages, providing quality and value to consumers at nearly 7,300 retail shops in almost 50 countries.

HISTORY

Beginning in 1945 the rich history of Baskin-Robbins starts with two brothers-in-laws' mutual love of ice cream. One of the cofounders, Irv Robbins, worked in his father's ice cream shop as a teen, while the other, Burton "Burt" Baskin, produced ice cream for his fellow troops in the U.S. Navy during World War II. After Burt returned from the war, the two ice cream enthusiasts knew they wanted to continue to brighten Americans' lives with delicious ice cream.

The entrepreneurial pair based their business vision on a love for old-fashioned ice cream and the desire to create a family-friendly location in local neighborhoods. They started out in separate ventures, running a shared total of six ice cream shops across Southern California. As the number of shops grew, Burt and Irv hired managers who could bring ownership interest and personal creativity to each location. Their management model pioneered the concept of franchising in the ice cream industry and still informs the hands-on approach that Baskin-Robbins utilizes today.

In 1949 Burt and Irv purchased their first dairy production facility, in Burbank, California. Controlling the production of their ice cream allowed them to experiment with new ingredients and flavors. In 1953 their separate shops merged into "Baskin-Robbins 31 Ice Cream," a brand that spotlights the unique concept of offering one ice cream flavor for each day of the month. The 31-flavors design represented the founders' commitment to personalizing the ice cream experience for their guests. As Irv Robbins once said, "Not everyone likes all our flavors, but each flavor is someone's favorite."

By the mid-1960s, Baskin-Robbins had expanded to more than 400 restaurants in the United States. The chain went international in the 1970s — opening shops in Japan, Saudi Arabia, Korea, and Australia — and is headquartered in Canton, Massachusetts, under its parent company, Dunkin' Brands Group Inc.

THE PRODUCT

Since 1945 Baskin-Robbins has introduced more than 1,200 fun and delicious flavors of hard-scoop ice cream to its Flavor Library. From

classic flavors like Pralines 'n Cream, which Irv Robbins created with his wife, Irma, in their California home kitchen in 1970, to more recent additions like French Toast, which was created by the award-winning Baskin-Robbins culinary team, Baskin-Robbins continues to lead the ice cream industry in flavor innovation. Baskin-Robbins also develops flavors for its international markets that cater to local palates, such as Green Tea in Asia. The brand's Rum Raisin ice cream contains real Jamaican rum in the United Kingdom.

The brand's launch of soft serve in 2008 cemented its status as the largest national chain to offer both hard-scoop ice cream and soft serve. In addition to its hard-scoop ice cream and soft-serve products, Baskin-Robbins offers its guests a wide range of frozen treats,

GREEN FOCUS

Environmental friendliness has always been a top priority for Baskin-Robbins. Baskin-Robbins switched to 100 percent postconsumer fiber napkins and usage-controlling dispensers in 2009. Together, these resulted in a 25 percent reduction in napkin waste overall. The company also switched to a recyclable pink spoon in 2014, an iconic representation of the decades-old ice cream brand.

including ice cream sundaes, custom ice cream cakes, take-home novelties like its Clown Cone, and a wide range of frozen beverages, which include its Cappuccino Blast®, Fruit Blasts, and smoothies.

Baskin-Robbins introduced a whole new way for ice cream lovers to enjoy ice cream cake when it unveiled its lineup of ice cream Cake Bites, which are elegant, ganache-coated mini desserts that combine ice cream and cake into a single serving. Baskin-Robbins ice cream Cake Bites allow guests to enjoy the indulgence of ice cream cake in a miniature, individual portion that's easy to grab and go.

RECENT DEVELOPMENTS
Despite its now-global presence, Baskin-Robbins strives to offer its guests around the world an inviting, neighborhood-ice-cream-shop feel at all of its restaurants. The company has opened its first restaurants in Vietnam, and the brand's presence is expanding in the United Kingdom and Mexico. As Baskin-Robbins grows around the world, it brings its classic lineup of delicious ice cream flavors to even more guests.

In recent years, Baskin-Robbins has focused on balancing dessert-time indulgence with better-for-you frozen treats. The BRight Choices® lineup of better-for-you options includes Berry Fruitful Greek Frozen Yogurt, Fat-Free Vanilla Frozen Yogurt, and No-Sugar-Added Brownie Sundae Ice Cream. These lighter options maintain the creativity, quality, and great taste that guests have come to expect from Baskin-Robbins.

PROMOTION
Throughout its storied history, Baskin-Robbins has embodied the friendly atmosphere of old-fashioned ice cream parlors and other fun pastimes, such as carnivals and cartoons. The company brings its flavors alive with a bright color palette, creative names, and delicious flavor ribbons and mix-ins. Baskin-Robbins restaurants also offers guests a free sample of any flavor available in the shop with its iconic pink spoon, so that they can try new flavors, including the brand's Flavor of the Month.

Over the past 70-plus years, the playful and creative spirit of Baskin-Robbins has captured holidays and notable moments in American history through ice cream flavors. It commemorated the relocation of the Dodgers from Brooklyn to Los Angeles in 1957 with Baseball Nut, and gave a nod to Beatlemania with Beatle Nut in 1964. When the first astronauts set foot on the moon in 1969, Lunar Cheesecake landed in Baskin-Robbins shops across the United States. On Valentine's Day 1995, Baskin-Robbins introduced Love Potion #31® to dipping cabinets nationwide, a flavor that has become a perennial favorite among guests.

BRAND VALUES
Baskin-Robbins' goal is to make its restaurants inviting, fun places to enjoy quality ice cream. The brand also reaches out to the neighborhood beyond its ice cream shops, hoping to share its optimistic outlook and charitable values with the community. In 2006 Dunkin' Brands established the Dunkin Donuts & Baskin-Robbins Community Foundation (DDBRCF), which initiates social action through food for the hungry, safety, and children's health initiatives.

July is National Ice Cream Month, Baskin-Robbins' favorite month of the year, and 2016 marked the USO's 75th anniversary. To honor this anniversary and Baskin-Robbins' commitment to supporting the U.S. military, the company held a special nationwide donation program on National Ice Cream Day and offered guests the new USO Patriot Pop flavor, which features cherry, lemon, and blue raspberry-flavored ices.

Baskin-Robbins donated 75 cents from every ice cream float sold on that date to the USO in honor of its 75th anniversary. The donations go toward supporting the USO's mission of connecting America's military to their family, home, and country, no matter the circumstances.

THINGS YOU DIDN'T KNOW ABOUT BASKIN-ROBBINS

○ Famous former Baskin-Robbins scoopers include U.S. president Barack Obama; chef Bobby Flay; actresses Julia Roberts, Rosie O'Donnell, and Chandra Wilson; actors Eric Dane and Randy Quaid; and TV host Leeza Gibbons.

○ There are more than 7,600 Baskin-Robbins locations around the world, with more than 2,500 located in the United States. Outside of the United States, Baskin-Robbins' largest markets include Japan and Korea, which each have nearly 1,200 locations.

○ Baskin-Robbins' top-selling ice cream flavors are Vanilla, Chocolate, Mint Chocolate Chip, Pralines 'n Cream, and Chocolate Chip. Pralines 'n Cream outsells Vanilla internationally.

Big Brothers Big Sisters of America

HISTORY

Chartered by Congress, Continued with Caring Adults

For more than a century, Big Brothers Big Sisters has helped children reach their potential. It all started in 1904, when a young New York City court clerk watched boy after boy pass through his courtroom. He believed that the help of caring adults could help many of these kids get on the right path, and he set out to find men who would guide them. That was the beginning of the Big Brothers movement.

A group called Ladies of Charity was taking a similar approach around the same time, linking adult women with girls who had ended up in the New York Children's Court. Eventually, Ladies of Charity evolved into Catholic Big Sisters. Congress chartered the Big Brothers Association in 1958. Both the Big Brothers and Big Sisters groups continued to work independently until 1977, when Big Brothers Association and Big Sisters International united to become Big Brothers Big Sisters of America.

More than 110 years later, Big Brothers Big Sisters remains true to its founders' vision of bringing supportive role models (Bigs) into the lives of children (Littles), ages six to 18, across the country in mentoring relationships (matches). Today, approximately 300 Big Brothers Big Sisters affiliates operate in all 50 states and serve more than 170,000 children, families, and volunteers. Across the globe, Big Brothers Big Sisters' impact can be felt in 21 other countries.

Recently, Big Brothers Big Sisters of America President and CEO and former mayor of Tampa Pam Iorio committed to leading the organization

through 2021. Tampa Bay businesses and community leaders have welcomed the organization to the area, where it expects to experience long-term growth.

Big Michael and Little Kaleb, Central Indiana

This country continues to have a need for adult mentors, and the strength of Big Brothers Big Sisters of America's brand is critical. Over the past year, the organization has adopted a mantra of "Moving Forward, Together" to describe this pivotal time of growth and collaboration.

ACHIEVEMENTS

Achieving Measurable Outcomes across the Country

Everything Big Brothers Big Sisters of America does starts with a Little. The organization is dedicated to researching and refining its practices for reaching more children, enriching the relationships those children have with their mentors, and extending the impact to underserved populations.

Workplace Mentoring with Corporate Partners. Big Brothers Big Sisters has three main programs: School-Based Mentoring, Community-Based Mentoring, and Workplace Mentoring. The newest initiative, Workplace Mentoring, makes it easy for companies and their employees to give back. Typically, local Big Brothers Big Sisters affiliates provide transportation for Littles so that they can meet with their Bigs at their Bigs' workplaces. The local affiliates monitor and support the one-to-one relationships with the same energy and effort as they do with the Community-Based and School-Based Mentoring programs.

Workplace Mentoring has given companies the chance to introduce Littles to career opportunities and aspirations; these partnerships have led to cobranding opportunities and helped foster new corporate brand ambassadors as well.

Warner Bros. Entertainment Partnerships. Over the past few years, Big Brothers Big Sisters has partnered with Warner Bros. Entertainment on films featuring strong mentor relationships. The partnership with the blockbuster movie *Creed* launched a national call for adults to become mentors through the Define Your Legacy campaign. The organization partnered with *The Hobbit* to play off of the big and little relationships in that film to emphasize the theme of "Whether You Are Big or Little, Start Something Epic."

Bowl for Kids' Sake. More than half a million people across America come together each year to have fun, bowl some strikes, and support the vital work of Big Brothers Big Sisters through its Bowl for Kids' Sake events. The design themes differ each year, but Bowl for Kids' Sake continues to be Big Brothers Big Sisters' largest fundraising effort.

BIG Champions Celebrity Ambassadors. Big Brothers Big Sisters of America recently launched its BIG Champions program, which features celebrity ambassadors who span geographic and demographic boundaries to speak to a variety of audiences. These BIG Champions include Pittsburgh Steelers player Antonio Brown;

Tampa Bay Buccaneers player Lavonte David; singer/songwriter LeToya Luckett, who was a founding member of Destiny's Child; singer/songwriter Eric Hutchinson; actor and comedian Jamie Foxx; MSNBC anchor Kate Snow; and actor Ryan Potter, star of Disney's *Big Hero 6*.

LEGACY
A BIG Need and a BIG Solution
The legacy of Big Brothers Big Sisters lives on through the lives and communities changed through mentorship. For decades, communities have seen the cyclical power of mentorship best demonstrated when former Littles continue the life-changing process of mentorship by eventually becoming Bigs.

"If someone doesn't put a vision in your life, or take you places you've never been, or show you things you've never seen, how can you dream any bigger?"

—Darryl, former Little Brother, now Big Brother

Although the Big Brothers Big Sisters brand is strong, its legacy relies on constant recruitment in order to continue to deliver on its promise of changing lives. Even as nonprofits and communities change, Big Brothers Big Sisters' unique one-to-one mentorship model and history of match support makes it more important than ever before.

A Big Need. As families become increasingly busy and as crime rates soar in certain communities, Big Brothers Big Sisters knows that mentorship can help steer youth to the right path. The need for mentorship programs is clear:

- Over 35 million youth in the United States are considered to be at risk of engaging in negative behaviors as a result of facing adversity.

- 54 percent of first-time drug users are under 18 years of age.

- 45 percent of children live in low-income families.

- Nearly one-third of black and Hispanic children are not graduating high school.

A Big Solution. By providing an extra layer of support, Big Brothers Big Sisters' highly monitored matches are proven to achieve measurable outcomes, such as educational success, avoidance of risky behaviors, higher aspirations, greater confidence, and better relationships. Research shows that when Bigs mentor Littles through Big Brothers Big Sisters, Littles are

- More confident

- Better decision-makers

- 52 percent less likely to skip school

- 46 percent less likely to begin using illegal drugs

- 27 percent less likely to begin using alcohol

Big Carrie and Little Regina, Tri-State, West Virginia

LOOKING AHEAD
Collaboration Fueling Change
Positively impacting the lives of children through mentoring is a team effort, and collaboration is at the core of Big Brothers Big Sisters' brand future. Through partnerships with local, state, and federal governments, corporations, foundations, and celebrities, Big Brothers Big Sisters will successfully recruit more mentors, educate more families, and serve more children throughout the country.

Government. Partnerships at every level of government are essential for Big Brothers Big Sisters. At the federal level, the Department of Justice and the Office of Juvenile Justice and Delinquency Prevention have been important partners for many years. Additionally, a partnership with the Department of Labor has led to the success of a program focused on transitioning young people into the workforce straight out of high school.

Foundations. By partnering with foundations, Big Brothers Big Sisters can focus on serving specific populations and further educational efforts such as STEM initiatives. This year, at the encouragement of the White House, Big Brothers Big Sisters also launched a partnership with the Take Our Daughters and Sons to Work Foundation, which will help more children experience a workplace with a strong adult role model.

Corporate Partners. Many Big Brothers Big Sisters' corporate partners commit their time or their financial or fundraising support to make a lasting impact on children's lives. Corporate partnerships, such as the partnership with Comcast NBCUniversal, are proof of how partnerships propel the Big Brothers Big Sisters mission. Since 2008 Comcast NBCUniversal has provided more than $65 million in cash and

in-kind support to Big Brothers Big Sisters, including airtime to broadcast public service announcements. Comcast hosts the largest workplace mentoring program, Beyond School Walls, with about 325 company employees volunteering as Bigs in 16 cities.

Brand Strategy. As a century-old national brand, Big Brothers Big Sisters of America will undergo an evolution as it approaches strategic planning and brand studies. To support this pivotal time in the brand's history, it has engaged the brand and marketing experts ChappellRoberts to continue to raise awareness, recruit mentors, and fundraise in order to ultimately serve more children across the country.

▶ **Classic Facts and Anecdotes**

- **Big Brothers Big Sisters is the nation's oldest and largest donor- and volunteer-supported mentoring network.**

- **Although Big Brothers Big Sisters agencies are able to serve 170,000 children, there are still 30,000 waiting for a strong adult role model.**

- **Artist Norman Rockwell completed a drawing for the organization in 1948 that became one of the best-known trademarks ever used by a social service organization.**

- **Each year, Big Brothers Big Sisters of America honors the top national Big Brother and Big Sister of the Year mentors—a tradition that began in 1950 and has been celebrated by President Dwight D. Eisenhower and President Lyndon B. Johnson.**

HISTORY

The Joseph A. Campbell Preserve Company was formed in 1869 by two men: Joseph Campbell and an icebox manufacturer named Abraham Anderson. The men started their business in Camden, New Jersey, where *Campbell's* world headquarters is still located. The original company produced canned tomatoes, vegetables, jellies, soups, condiments, and minced meats. But in 1897, twenty-four-year-old Dr. John T. Dorrance made a discovery that would change the company's focus — and fortune — forever. Dr. Dorrance invented condensed soup, which allows a high-quality product to be produced and shipped relatively inexpensively while simultaneously saving space on retail shelves and in consumers' cupboards. After the company began an extensive nationwide taste test to allow housewives the opportunity of tasting the new soup, the product became a household staple.

Ancillary products were soon dropped to allow the company to focus on the burgeoning condensed soup business. In 1922 the company's name was officially changed to Campbell Soup Company.

In 1934 *Campbell's* introduced the first soup to be used primarily as a sauce, expanding the product's usefulness in the kitchen. Cream of Mushroom soup went on to become one of the top-three-selling soups produced by Campbell. In 1955 Dorcas Reilly, a Campbell home economist, created a dish that

today is integrally tied to the holidays: Green Bean Casserole. This amazing sidedish, easily put together in just one cooking dish, has been served with millions of Thanksgiving dinners for more than half a century.

Campbell began production of *Campbell's* tomato juice in 1937, using its expertise in growing fine tomatoes to produce a quality beverage that would be available year round.

In 1962 *Campbell's* status as an American icon was solidified when pop artist Andy Warhol painted his famous *Campbell's* soup cans. When asked why he painted the iconic can, Warhol once replied that he had eaten *Campbell's* soups once a day for 20 years.

Campbell's Chunky soup was introduced in 1970, creating a successful lineup of hearty, ready-to-eat soups.

In 1981 *Prego* Italian sauce came on the market, expanding Campbell further into the simple meals category.

In 2006 *V8 V-Fusion,* a beverage made from 100 percent vegetable and fruit juices, was launched, successfully combining two healthy servings of fruits and vegetables into one great taste. Each eight-ounce glass provides a full serving of vegetables and a full serving of fruit with a delicious taste.

Promotion. In 1899 John Dorrance took a gamble in New York City when he was the first manufacturer to place advertising on New York City's streetcars. The ads featured a large illustration of the iconic *Campbell's* condensed soup can. Sales in New York City increased by 100 percent in just two years.

A few years later another icon was "born." *The Campbell Kids,* illustrated by Grace Wiederseim, made their appearance on streetcars in Philadelphia in 1904. They became hugely

popular and have been included in *Campbell's* advertising and reproduced on thousands of licensed pieces around the world.

The famous *"M'm! M'm! Good!"* jingle was created in 1931 for a radio spot. The company sponsored some of the classic radio shows, including the *George Burns and Gracie Allen Show* and the *Campbell's Showcase*. The song has been incorporated into *Campbell's* advertising in various ways for more than eight decades,

including the recent "So Many, Many Reasons it's so . . . *M'm! M'm! Good!*" campaign for condensed soup.

ACHIEVEMENTS

In 1897 the Joseph A. Campbell Preserve Company introduced a food revolution: condensed soups. Dr. John T. Dorrance, nephew of the company's general manager, invented this new way of producing soup. By adding less water right from the start, Dorrance significantly lowered the cost of packaging, shipping, and storage. This innovation allowed the Joseph A. Campbell Preserve Company to offer a 10-ounce can for 10 cents, compared to more than 30 cents for a 32-ounce can of typical soup. Twenty-one varieties were soon available, and *Campbell's* quickly became the most successful soup brand, a position it has held for more than a century. More than 2.5 billion bowls of *Campbell's* soup — including Chicken Noodle, Tomato, and Cream of Mushroom — are consumed by Americans each year.

In 1916 *Campbell's* condensed soups began to be used in recipes. *Campbell's* Kitchen created a number of recipes that have been enjoyed on America's tables for

decades. Green Bean Casserole remains one of the staples of America's holiday tables after more than 50 years. More than 440 million cans of *Campbell's* soups are used in easy-to-prepare recipes in America each year. Cooking with *Campbell's* soup is so popular that the

product ranks behind only meat/poultry, pasta, and seasonings/spices as the ingredient most frequently used to prepare dinner each evening.

Beyond soups, Campbell owns some of the world's most recognizable brands. *Pepperidge Farm* bread, cookies, and crackers in the United States and *Arnott's* cookies and crackers in Australia are two of the strongest players in the baked snacks marketplace. *Erasco* and *Liebig* are successful brands in Europe. *V8* 100% vegetable juice is among the most popular vegetable juices in the world. *Swanson* broth consistently ranks in the top five of products purchased during holiday time. Prego Italian sauces is one of America's most popular brands of Italian sauces. (The recipe is actually based on a family-favorite recipe of one of *Campbell's* chefs, using spices imported from around the world.) *Pace* Mexican sauces was acquired in 1995; *Pace* Picante sauce is still made using the recipe David Pace developed more than 60 years ago. The portfolio of brands and geographies has grown such that Campbell products are now sold in approximately 120 countries around the globe.

LEGACY

The choices that America's families have for a nutritious, simple meal are varied and vast, but one staple that parents have been serving for more than a century is *Campbell's* soups. The *Campbell's* trademark and the brands under its banner are true American icons, imbued with rich collective and individual emotion. While *Campbell's* U.S. soups remain the largest business in the company, Campbell has other leading soup brands around the world, including *Campbell's* Gardennay in Canada, *Liebig* and *Royco* in France and Belgium, *Erasco* and *Heisse*

Tasse in Germany, and *Campbell's* in Australia, New Zealand, and Hong Kong.

However, Campbell is not just a soup company. Over the years the company has acquired or developed other important market-leading positions. All of the company's brands share three commonalities: each is unique, iconic, and a powerful marketing force.

Health initiatives. *Campbell's* continues its sponsorship with the American Heart Association as well as its support of the Go Red For Women movement. As a national supporter of Go Red For Women, *Campbell's* has pledged over $5.4 million to the cause through 2015. *Campbell's* diverse portfolio of products include over 70 options that meet the criteria for the American Heart Association's Heart-Check Mark.

LOOKING AHEAD

Campbell Soup Company has created a truly American icon in the Campbell's trademark. The Campbell's trademark embodies an emotional dimension that resonates with America's families. With a taste that adults and children both love, Campbell's extols family values with trustworthy, quality products.

▶ **Classic Facts and Anecdotes**

- Americans purchase more than 70 cans of *Campbell's* soups every second.

- Tomato was the first variety of soup created by Campbell.

- The *Campbell Kids* celebrated their 110th birthday in 2014.

- The genesis of the red and white color design on *Campbell's* condensed soup cans came after a company executive attended a Cornell University football game. The executive was so taken by the team's new red and white uniforms that he convinced Campbell to use the colors on its labels.

HISTORY

Originally named Binney & Smith, Crayola was established when cousins Edwin Binney and C. Harold Smith took over Edwin's father's pigment business in 1885. Early products included red oxide pigment used in barn paint and carbon black for car tires.

Listening to the needs of teachers, Binney & Smith made the first dustless school chalk in 1902. After noticing a need for safe, high-quality, affordable wax crayons, the company produced the first box of eight Crayola crayons

in 1903 and sold them for five cents. The Crayola name, coined by Edwin Binney's wife, Alice, comes from *craie*, the French word for chalk, and "ola," from "oleaginous," meaning oily.

The first 64-count Crayola crayon box with the built-in sharpener was introduced in 1958, and the company sold the first box of Crayola markers in 1978.

In 1984 Binney & Smith became a wholly owned subsidiary of Hallmark Cards Inc. of Kansas City, Missouri — the world's leader in social expression. The company celebrated its centennial in 2003.

Reflecting the company's number-one-brand status, Binney & Smith changed its name to Crayola in 2007. Crayola continues to grow, adding innovative products based on consumer insights, quality, and safety: values the company has held since its inception.

ACHIEVEMENTS

Crayons, markers, pencils, and notebooks have long been the basic school supplies in kids'

backpacks on the first day of school. Crayola then added a new essential to back-to-school

lists — dry-erase tools. As whiteboards replace chalkboards in classrooms across the United States and students are using smaller versions in class, dry-erase usage for learning and creative at-home fun is on the rise. Crayola created dry-erase tools that are washable and smudge-proof, have no odor, and will never dry out.

Crayola Washable Dry-Erase Bright Crayons come in eight intensely bold colors, including white for drawing and writing on black dry-erase surfaces. A machine-washable "E-Z Erase" cloth comes in each pack for easily wiping dry-erase surfaces clean, and Crayola's classic built-in crayon sharpener is on the back, so tips are always ready for action.

In addition to crayons, markers, and colored pencils, Crayola products include Model Magic®, Color Wonder®, chalk, outdoor products, My First Crayola®, clay, paint, and Silly Putty®.

Over the years, Crayola has introduced innovations such as washability, erasability, 3D, and messfree capability. Crayola washable products — such as washable crayons, markers, and paint — are specially formulated to easily wash from skin and most children's clothing. The company's Color Wonder® products are clear, with color appearing only on Color Wonder paper, not on clothes, walls, skin, or furniture.

Products are sold in more than 80 countries and packaged in 12 languages: English, French, Dutch, German, Italian, Spanish, Portuguese, Danish, Finnish, Japanese, Swedish, and Norwegian.

LEGACY

Crayola aspires to help parents and teachers raise creative and inspired kids. The brand believes in giving children an invitation that ignites, colors that inspire, and tools that transform original thought into visible form. It's important to unleash, nurture, and celebrate the

colorful originality in every child — to give colorful wings to the invisible things in young people's hearts and minds.

Crayola also believes that an investment in the community is an investment in the company itself and in its employees. The company is committed to the role of corporate citizen in the Lehigh Valley of Pennsylvania. Hundreds of employees volunteer among numerous nonprofit organizations each year. Crayola provides cash and product donations to more than 300 nonprofit arts, education, and health and welfare organizations annually within the Lehigh Valley.

The company is also committed to continual revitalization of downtown Easton. The Crayola Experience, a 20,000-square-foot hands-on discovery center at Two Rivers Landing, opened in 1996 in Easton and has brought more than 4 million visitors to the area. The Crayola Experience specializes in creative and imaginative fun for kids of all ages. In addition to seeing the manufacture of Crayola crayons and markers, visitors can experience dozens of hands-on exhibits and activities that encourage outside-the-lines thinking and playing.

Through the years, kids, creativity, color, and fun have remained the cornerstones of Crayola. According to Smarty Pants, an annual brand tracking study of U.S. family-friendly brands, Crayola in 2015 was the seventh-highest-ranking brand among mothers of children ages six to 12.

LOOKING AHEAD

Even though Crayola had long been a leader in crayons, markers, and pencils, in 2004 the decision was made to become more than what's inside a little yellow box at back-to-school time. Crayola moved to become an innovative brand that places unlimited opportunity for expression into the hands of children to nurture the power of creativity all year long.

"The Art of Childhood" campaign grew from the idea that the art of imagination is a natural part of being a child and raising a child.

In 2008 the company launched a broad media campaign to position Crayola products as the ideal gift for the holidays. A series of commercials, a multipage print campaign, and an online gift guide successfully made the holiday season a rival to back-to-school time as a top-selling season. Crayola then launched "Everything Imaginable" in 2009.

Now, with coordinated campaigns occurring several times a year, Crayola is truly becoming a brand that provides everything children need to express themselves.

▶ Classic Facts and Anecdotes

- Since its debut in 1958 on *Captain Kangaroo,* more than 200 million Crayola 64 boxes, holding 13 billion crayons, have been sold. All those crayons would circle the earth 24 times.

- According to a Yale University study, the smell of a fresh box of Crayola crayons is among the 20 most recognizable scents to American adults. Coffee and peanut butter are numbers 1 and 2; Crayola crayons are number 18.

THE MARKET

The U.S. dentifrice market is highly competitive, fueled by improved benefits and new product introductions. According to the latest available statistics, the paste category accounted for approximately $3 billion in annual sales and is growing at 1 to 2 percent per year. The market is segmented into base and premium, with base products offering cavity and tartar protection and premium products offering multiple benefits and whitening. The premium segment is driving category growth as consumers seek new and improved products.

ACHIEVEMENTS

Crest has been a leader in oral-care innovations since its introduction in 1955 and has been the leading toothpaste brand in the United States over the past 60 years. In 1976 the American Chemical Society recognized Crest with fluoride as one of the 100 greatest discoveries of the previous 100 years. In 1999 Crest was the first whitening toothpaste to receive the ADA Seal of Acceptance. In 2006 Crest received another ADA seal of acceptance for its Pro-Health toothpaste.

HISTORY

The development of fluoride toothpaste began in the early 1940s when Procter & Gamble started a research program to find ingredients that would reduce tooth decay when added to a dentifrice.

At that time, Americans developed an estimated 700 million cavities a year, making dental disease one of the most prevalent U.S. health problems. In 1950 Procter & Gamble developed a joint research project team led by Dr. Joseph Muhler at Indiana University to study a new toothpaste with fluoride. The study's startling results indicated that children ages six to 16 showed an average 49 percent reduction in cavities, and adults showed tooth decay reduction to almost the same degree. In 1954 Procter & Gamble submitted the results of its extensive testing to the American Dental Association. Test marketing of Crest with Fluoristan began in 1955. While initial sales were disappointing, Crest moved forward with the national launch in January 1956. On

August 1, 1960, the ADA reported, "Crest has been shown to be an effective anticaries (decay preventative) dentifrice that can be of significant value when used in a conscientiously applied program of oral hygiene and regular professional care." The response was electric. Within a year, Crest's sales nearly doubled. By 1962 they had nearly tripled, pushing Crest well ahead as the best-selling toothpaste in the United States.

In 2001 Crest revolutionized at-home whitening with the launch of Crest Whitestrips®, the first-ever patented strip technology designed to whiten teeth in 14 days. The unique strip format conforms to the shape of teeth, utilizing the same enamel-safe ingredient that dentists use.

In April 2005 Crest introduced its first mouthwash, Crest Pro-Health Oral Rinse. The formulation is alcohol-free and has been shown in laboratory tests to kill 99 percent of common germs that can cause plaque, gingivitis, and bad breath — all without the burn of alcohol.

Crest provides oral health resources and education through product donation to dental clinics, as well as first-grade and pediatrician education, and works with nonprofits like Operation Smile.

THE PRODUCT

Crest's heritage is grounded in the dentifrice market, but the company has expanded into many

Crest. Major Moments

1955
Crest launches its first clinically proven fluoride toothpaste with "Look, Mom – no cavities!" campaign.

1960
ADA reports that Crest effectively prevents tooth decay.

ADA

1976
American Chemical Society lists Crest's fluoride toothpaste as one of the great discoveries of the past 100 years.

A C S

1980s
Several ingredient breakthroughs fortify the trusted Crest brand with benefits like tartar control and cavity-fighting protection.

1990s
Crest adds the beauty benefit of whitening to its trusted oral-health formulas.

2000
Crest Healthy Smiles is established to improve the state of oral health.

Crest Healthy Smiles

Healthy, Beautiful Smiles for Life

2001
Crest launches Crest Whitestrips, a revolutionary product in the whitening and oral care industry.

Crest Whitestrips

2003
Crest acquires Glide floss and the number-one dentist-recommended floss joins the Crest family. Crest launches Whitening Expressions, a line of whitening tooth-pastes with unique flavors that enhance the everyday brushing experience.

Crest Glide

2005
Crest celebrates its 50th anniversary of bringing Healthy Beautiful Smiles to Life. Crest launches its first mouth rinse, Crest Pro-Health Rinse, that kills plaque, gingivitis, and bad breath germs "without the burn" of alcohol.

other oral-care product lines as well. Crest now offers a broad range of products for dental needs and conducts the nation's best-known activities on behalf of good dental practices among children.

Since its inception, Crest has led the way in dental health innovations and improving oral health. Today, Crest is among the most trusted household brands in the United States. Crest has evolved its active ingredients to offer different options based on individual need. For example, Crest Pro-Health uses stannous fluoride and offers protection against plaque and gingivitis. Crest 3D White uses sodium fluoride and helps reveal your smile's whiteness by removing surface stains. Finally, Crest Complete offers toothpaste the whole family will enjoy, plus the protection you'd expect from any Crest product.

RECENT DEVELOPMENTS

Benefitting from Crest's continuous product development and improvement, customers can now enjoy Crest's HD daily two-step system, which isolates ingredients to deliver superior results with a Purifying Cleanser and Perfecting Gel. Step 1 strips plaque away, and Step 2 polishes and whitens for an experience that lets you feel the difference from first use. The results are a more luminescent smile with superior cleaning, whitening, and sensitivity relief at two weeks. Each system contains one 4-ounce Step 1 tube and one 2.3-ounce Step 2 tube.

Healthier smiles make a difference to Crest, and there's no better time to start good oral health care than in the younger years. Statistics show that children with poor oral health are nearly three times more likely to miss school, and kids with toothaches are nearly four times more likely to have a lower grade point average. A study has shown that more than 51 million school hours are lost annually due to dental-related illness. Parents who are concerned about the amount of time their kids brush can download a free Disney Magic Timer app by Oral-B; with this app, even the most reluctant children brush longer. To unlock the fun, all a family needs is a Crest or Oral-B Pro-Health Stages or Jr. product.

Crest/Oral-B and the AAO (American Association of Orthodontists) teamed up in 2015 to raise awareness about good oral hygiene maintenance for orthodontic patients in addition to the benefits of getting professional services from AAO member orthodontists. "Orthodontic treatment is a smart investment in good dental health," according to Morris N. Poole, DDS, president of the AAO. "Good oral hygiene is especially critical during orthodontic treatment. Using the proper oral care products can help patients keep teeth and gums clean, and enjoy a healthy and beautiful smile when their treatment is complete."

Crest + Oral-B's collaboration with the AAO includes a number of activities to build awareness among dental professionals as well as consumers, including the development of materials to help dental professionals communicate and engage their patients on oral hygiene techniques and making the right product choices for optimal oral health.

Crest/Oral-B is one of the global leaders in oral care product technologies with the most comprehensive range of home care products, such as Bluetooth-enabled electric toothbrushes, toothpastes, rinses, flosses, and other specialty products. Its Ortho Essentials Kit has been scientifically shown to reduce plaque and improve oral health in patients who are having orthodontic treatment.

PROMOTION

Crest has a significant social media presence, showing that the brand knows its audience and how to navigate the forever-changing social media world. As of summer 2016, Crest's Facebook page had over 1 million likes. Crest also used its Facebook page to celebrate the bronze-winning performance of Canadian heptathlete and Crest ambassador Brianne Theisen-Eaton in the Rio Olympic Games. During the Games, Laurie Hernandez, U.S. Olympic gymnastics gold and silver medalist, was named the Crest and Orgullosa ambassador. Laurie's mother, Wanda Hernandez, also joined the "Thank You Mom" family to share her journey and highlight the pivotal role moms play in the children's health and well-being. The breakthrough Olympic Games star and her mother will be featured alongside Crest in a campaign on the Orgullosa online platform, which was created to celebrate, empower, and fuel Latinas' accomplishments and dreams.

BRAND VALUES

Crest is a brand that has continually pushed to improve oral health. Crest is among the most trusted household brands, a value reinforced by the continued recognition of its products by the American Dental Association. Crest's dream is to lead the way in the passionate pursuit of perfect oral health so that everyone can have a healthy, beautiful smile for life.

THINGS YOU DIDN'T KNOW ABOUT CREST

○ Within two years of its ADA acceptance, Crest's sales nearly tripled, pushing Crest well ahead as the best-selling toothpaste in the United States.

○ To date, there are a total of 100+ active open-stock national SKUs of Crest toothpaste, which includes all SKU sizes.

2006
Crest launches Crest Pro-Health, the first toothpaste to protect against all seven areas dentists check: gingivitis, plaque, cavities, tartar, sensitivity, stains, and fresh breath. Crest launches Crest Whitestrips Renewal in response to the ever-growing anti-aging trend.

2009
Crest introduces Crest Whitestrips Advanced Seal. The groundbreaking adhesive formulation temporarily molds the strip to users' teeth, allowing them to easily talk and drink water for convenient whitening anywhere, anytime.

2010
The Crest and Oral-B 3D White collection (Whitestrips, toothpaste, mouthwash, toothbrushes), together provide noticeable whitening results in one day. Crest Pro-Health™ Sensitive Shield Toothpaste guards against teeth sensitivity while providing comprehensive protection for teeth and gums.

2011
Crest & Oral-B introduce the Complete product portfolio, an offering of toothpastes, mouthwashes, toothbrushes, and flosses. Specifically, Scope Dual-Blast mouthwash features a unique dual-action technology that not only kills 98 percent of bad-breath germs, but blasts away strong food odors.

2012
Crest 3D White introduces Luxe Glamorous White Toothpaste and Intensive Professional Effects Whitestrips. Crest 3D White Luxe Glamorous White Toothpaste removes up to 90 percent of surface stains in five days and delivers brighter teeth in one day. Crest 3D White Intensive Professional Effects Whitestrips deliver visibly whiter teeth after just one use by removing stains below the enamel's surface.

2013
Crest 3D White introduces Luxe Lustrous Shine Toothpaste, Luxe Sensitivity Toothpaste, and 1 Hour Express Whitestrips. Crest 3D White Luxe Sensitivity Toothpaste contains an enamel-safe whitening ingredient and fights tooth sensitivity with regular brushing. Crest 3D White Whitestrips 1 Hour Express removes years of stains after just a single one-hour treatment, further exhibiting Crest's innovation in the whitening space.

WELCOME TO AMERICA'S DINER®

THE MARKET

Denny's is widely known as America's Diner. For more than 60 years, this classic restaurant chain has served as a local gathering spot in the community. Offering a warm, comfortable, and friendly environment, Denny's is always open and ready to welcome its guests in for a great meal at a reasonable price.

With its iconic yellow signs dotting America's highways, cities, and towns, Denny's greets its guests with the consistent promise of variety, comfort, and hospitality. It does so with a wink and a smile and a friendly wisecrack over a never-empty cup of coffee. Best known for its all-day signature items, such as the Original Grand Slam,® Moons Over My Hammy,® Sizzlin' Skillets, hand-dipped Milk Shakes, 100% Beef Burgers, and Pancake Puppies,® Denny's offers guests a place to sit back, relax, and enjoy classic American comfort food and everyday value, 24 hours a day, 365 days a year.

ACHIEVEMENTS

As America's Diner, Denny's is committed to celebrating an internal and external brand culture that promotes an openness to all people, ideas, and perspectives. The brand firmly believes that a diverse workplace is a strong workplace and should reflect the communities it serves. As of 2016, minorities make up 65 percent of Denny's total workforce and 51 percent of overall management. The Denny's Board of Directors consists of 10 members, of whom 50 percent are minorities and/or women. Over the years, Denny's diversity progress has been widely acknowledged by civil rights leaders, community groups, and many publications, including *Fortune, Hispanic Business, Black Enterprise, Asian Enterprise, Family Digest,* and *Minority Business News USA.* In addition, Denny's has been recognized as one of the top companies to work for by *Latino Magazine, Black EOE Journal, Savoy Magazine,* and the Human Rights Campaign.

Furthermore, in order to strengthen partnerships with minority- and women-owned suppliers, Denny's initiated a Supplier

Diversity Program in 1993 and has spent more than $1.7 billion with minority-owned suppliers since the program's inception.

Denny's is also proud to help support the unique and diverse causes in the many communities it serves — from education initiatives and minority business conferences to childhood hunger programs and fundraisers.

Denny's Hungry for Education program helps promote and improve education throughout the nation by partnering with leading nonprofit minority advocacy organizations. Through the program, Denny's has presented more than $500,000 in combined scholarships to deserving students across the country. Additionally, Denny's continues its commitment to the fight against childhood hunger through its efforts with Share Our Strength's "No Kid Hungry®" campaign, a national movement aimed at ending childhood hunger. The brand has donated more than $4.3 million to date.

HISTORY

The restaurant chain now known as Denny's began in Lakewood, California, in 1953 with a dream and a doughnut stand called "Danny's Donuts." The owner, Harold Butler, started his business with a solid commitment: "We're going to serve the best cup of coffee, make the best doughnuts, give the best service, keep everything spotless, offer the best value, and stay open 24 hours a day." In 1959 when Butler had grown his business to 20 locations, he renamed it "Denny's Restaurants" to avoid confusion with another chain, "Doughnut Dan's." By 1963 the company's expansion success was attributed to a franchising program that pushed the chain to 78 restaurants across seven western states. This highly competitive program continues to be an important part of Denny's growth strategy today, as 92 percent of its restaurants are franchisee-owned.

During this significant growth period, Denny's realized that to separate itself from other expanding family dining chains, it needed to focus on offering personalized guest service and delivering unbeatable satisfaction. Denny's servers welcomed guests personally and focused on their individual needs and requirements.

Now in 2017, Denny's has grown from a small doughnut stand to one of the largest full-service family restaurant chains, with more than 1,700 locations across all 50 states and in 13 countries. Denny's unstoppable growth continues with further domestic and international expansion, while over 75 percent of all Denny's restaurants will be remodeled by the end of 2018 to reflect the brand's innovative diner development. Today, Denny's is truly a brand with unbeatable momentum.

THE PRODUCT

Over the years, Denny's has gained a cult association with its popular breakfast offerings like Moons Over My Hammy,® Supreme Skillet, and the world-famous Build Your Own Grand Slam,® with over 21 million sold in 2016. Its expansive menu features delicious, innovative options for appetizers, lunch, dinner, and dessert, any time of day. The wide variety of dishes also caters to the taste and dietary requirements of every guest who walks through its doors. So whether diners are in the mood to indulge in a Honey Jalapeño Bacon Sriracha Burger, Lumberjack Slam®, or Sticky Bun Pancake Breakfast, or prefer a lighter alternative such as the Fit Fare® Loaded Veggie Omelette, Fit Slam®, or Wild Alaska Salmon Skillet, the diner caters to every craving. Along with the 16-item $2 $4 $6 $8 Value Menu® and buzzworthy limited-time-only menus, evolving variety and taste play a key part in how Denny's continually develops its product line-ups to fit within its guests' ever-changing lifestyles.

and enhanced flavors, without compromising on the brand's signature taste, value, and variety. Since 2012, over 50 percent of Denny's menu and traditional recipes have been developed to meet guests' ever-evolving needs. Most recently, Denny's launched a new and improved Buttermilk Pancake recipe that includes fresh buttermilk, real eggs, and a hint of vanilla, resulting in tastier, better, and 50 percent fluffier pancakes. Along with new additions to the menu such as Honey Jalapeño Bacon and Hearty Breakfast Sausage, health-conscious options have been added to the classic Grand Slam,® including seasonal fruit, yogurt, turkey bacon, gouda-apple chicken sausage, and more. Denny's also serves USDA select beef, wild-caught and sustainable salmon, fresh-cut vegetables, seven-grain bread, and gluten-free English Muffins. Additionally, in

most iconic breakfast entrée, the Grand Slam,® to life. The web series *The Grand Slams* features the hijinks of Denny's anthropomorphized breakfast favorites and has garnered over 70 million completed views and a strong millennial following. Additionally, Denny's presence on Tumblr, Instagram, Facebook, Twitter, and YouTube has a combined social following of over 2 million fans and growing, garnering a plethora of recognized industry awards including Social Media Marketer of the Year from *Restaurant Business*.

BRAND VALUES

Denny's is shaped by a simple philosophy: We Love to Feed People.™ This is its purpose, what drives Denny's, and is the resounding rallying cry throughout the organization — from its team members in-restaurant to those working in the brand's corporate office. Denny's isn't just a place to feed people's appetites, but also a place that feeds the lives of its guests by giving them a place to share great conversations, a chance to get together with family and friends, and a place that feeds the body and the spirit of anyone who comes through the front doors.

RECENT DEVELOPMENTS

In coordination with its franchisee network, Denny's continues to invest in the overall guest experience — in-restaurant, online, and in the community. From contemporary location remodels and innovative restaurant guest technology to strategic partnerships with key brands such as 20th Century Fox, Warner Brothers, DreamWorks, AARP, and the Tom Joyner Foundation — Denny's is truly a brand on the move.

One of Denny's recent primary areas of focus has been on improved food quality, premium ingredients,

2016 the brand committed to sourcing and serving 100 percent cage-free eggs in all US restaurants by 2026.

PROMOTION

Denny's recognizes that marketing goes beyond traditional media, and it has positioned itself as an industry leader in the digital, mobile, and social marketplace. Targeting the modern American family where they live, work, and play, Denny's uses a diverse and premium list of media partners — such as Facebook, YouTube, Waze, Yelp, and Pandora — to pinpoint moments when its targets are most receptive to its message, connecting with them in a way that is relevant and engaging. Over the past couple of years, Denny's has created a quirky digital web video series bringing its

THE MARKET

Founded in 1950, Dunkin' Donuts is America's favorite all-day, everyday stop for coffee and baked goods. With more than 8,000 restaurants in 41 U.S. states plus the District of Columbia and more than 3,200 restaurants in 36 countries, Dunkin' Donuts global franchisee-reported sales were approximately $10.4 billion in 2015. As the number-one retailer of hot and iced coffee in America, the brand is also a market leader in the donut, bagel, breakfast sandwich, and muffin categories.

Enjoying a cup of Dunkin' Donuts coffee is a daily ritual for millions of people. The company serves approximately 1.7 billion cups of hot and iced coffee every year, and Dunkin' Donuts' standards for coffee excellence are among the best in the industry.

Beloved by generations and increasingly recognized by guests around the world, Dunkin' Donuts prides itself on serving consistently high-quality food and beverages that are fast, fresh, and affordably priced. This brand promise, combined with its healthy and profitable franchisee community, should enable Dunkin' Donuts to realize its plans to more than double its U.S. presence, expanding to 15,000 restaurants over the next two decades.

ACHIEVEMENTS

Dunkin' Donuts believes that its guests deserve the finest, highest-quality coffee in the industry. Taking cues from discriminating wine connoisseurs, the company conducts a "full sensory evaluation" of its Arabica roasted beans. The Dunkin' Donuts coffee experts taste an average of 200

cups of coffee each day to ensure that the product always meets its standards for coffee excellence. With attention to detail like this, it's no surprise that the Brand Keys Customer Loyalty Index in 2016 ranked Dunkin' Donuts as a top brand for consumer engagement in the out-of-home coffee category, the tenth consecutive year Dunkin' Donuts has earned this honor. Dunkin' Donuts also led the packaged coffee category in customer loyalty for the fourth year in a row. The company was also named one of the Top 10 Franchises for 2016 in *Entrepreneur* magazine, and made a strong showing in the 2016 American Customer Satisfaction Index (ACSI). According to the 2016 ACSI, Dunkin' Donuts offered a more satisfying customer experience than Starbucks.

Even as one of the fastest-growing quick-serve restaurants, Dunkin' Donuts is already the nation's number-one retailer of ready-brewed hot, regular, flavored, decaf, and iced coffee. Dunkin' Donuts coffee is also the number-one-selling premium bagged grocery coffee.

HISTORY

The story of Dunkin' Donuts begins in 1948, when William Rosenberg opened a donut and coffee restaurant called the Open Kettle in Quincy, Massachusetts. He served premium cups of coffee for ten cents and donuts for five cents. In 1950 Rosenberg renamed the restaurant to

Dunkin' Donuts after a brainstorming session with his team. As his architect enthusiastically reasoned, "What do you do with a donut? You dunk it!"

After the first Dunkin' Donuts franchise opened in 1955, the number of restaurants grew to 100 over the next decade. Just as the number of Dunkin' Donuts locations was expanding, so was the menu. Rosenberg expanded Dunkin' Donuts' offerings beyond donuts and coffee to

include Munchkin donut holes and muffins in 1978. Since then, the company has become known for its product innovation and has introduced a wide variety of delicious food and beverages, including iced coffee, freshly baked bagels, breakfast sandwiches, and more.

Rosenberg had a simple philosophy: "Make and serve the freshest, most delicious coffee and donuts quickly and courteously in modern, well-merchandised stores." This philosophy still holds true today and is the foundation that has enabled Dunkin' Donuts to grow into one of the world's most beloved brands. Based in Canton, Massachusetts, Dunkin' Donuts is a subsidiary of Dunkin' Brands Inc., which is also the parent company of sister brand Baskin-Robbins.

THE PRODUCT

Dunkin' Donuts serves "America's Favorite Coffee," as well as a wide variety of delicious food and beverages to keep guests running all day. Dunkin' Donuts coffee is available in eight flavors: blueberry, caramel, cinnamon, coconut, French vanilla, hazelnut, raspberry, and toasted almond. All flavorings are sugar-free and contain no preservatives. In 2004, Dunkin' Donuts partnered with Fair Trade USA to begin purchasing Fair Trade Certified coffee for its espresso. Dunkin'

Donuts was the first national brand to sell a full line of espresso beverages made exclusively with 100 percent Fair Trade Certified coffee. Along with coffee products, Dunkin' Donuts serves a host of other beverages, including hot chocolate, iced tea, and exclusive Coolatta® frozen drinks.

GREEN FOCUS

Over the past few years, Dunkin' Donuts has reduced the amount of waste that guests generate. For example, the napkins in U.S. Dunkin' Donuts restaurants are made with 100 percent recycled content and are recyclable, biodegradable, and compostable. In 2014, the company transitioned U.S. Dunkin' Donuts bagel bags to 100 percent recycled paper.

Dunkin' Donuts also offers guests the ability to choose from a wide variety of "better-for-you" selections. These better-for-you products are marketed as DDSMART®, making it easy for guests to select great-tasting food and beverages that fit their dietary wants and needs. Dunkin' Donuts' DDSMART menu features items such as the Multigrain Bagel, Reduced Fat Blueberry Muffin, and Egg White Veggie Flatbread. All DDSMART items have either fewer calories, less fat, less sugar, or more overall nutritional value than comparable fare.

Dunkin' Donuts takes special measures to ensure that guests can access their favorite products in a variety of locations beyond the restaurants. For example, Dunkin' Donuts has Dunkin' Donuts K-Cup® portion packs in a popular range of flavors, making "America's Favorite Coffee" available for use at home with the Keurig Single-Cup Brewing System and at the touch of a button. Dunkin' Donuts also has an exclusive partnership with JetBlue Airways, which allows JetBlue customers to enjoy Dunkin' Donuts products on-board all flights throughout America, including Decaf and Original Blend coffee, as well as Dunkin' Donuts Original and Green Tea.

RECENT DEVELOPMENTS

In August 2016, participating Dunkin' Donuts restaurants began offering Cold Brew coffee. Dunkin' Donuts' Cold Brew coffee is prepared by steeping a special blend of coffee in cold water over an extended period of time to extract a uniquely distinctive flavor from the beans. The longer brewing process provides a rich, smooth coffee with an inherently sweeter flavor, reminiscent of dark chocolate. Cold Brew offers another choice, along with the brand's signature iced coffee, for those who prefer their coffee cold. "The launch of Cold Brew coffee represents a bold new option for our coffee fans and an important addition to our lineup of quality, innovative beverages," according to Chris Fuqua, senior vice president, Dunkin' Donuts Brand Marketing, Global Consumer Insights & Product Innovation.

PROMOTION

The Dunkin' Donuts brand reflects the characteristics of its guests. Dunkin' Donuts serves high-quality food and beverages for busy people on the go — people who take what they do seriously, without taking themselves too seriously. Dunkin' Donuts' guests perceive themselves as authentic and true to themselves. They take pride in knowing who they are and where they come from; they truly make America run.

This understanding of its guests provided the foundation for Dunkin Donuts' acclaimed advertising campaign that was introduced in 2006: "America Runs on Dunkin'"®. In 2011, Dunkin' Donuts launched a successful extension of "America Runs on Dunkin'"®, which was anchored by a simple question and answer: "What are you drinkin'?" "I'm drinkin' Dunkin'."

The "What are you drinkin'?" ad campaign features "everyday Joes," from construction workers to soccer moms to accountants.

On National Donut Day in 2016, Dunkin' Donuts expanded its long-running "America Runs on Dunkin'"® campaign yet again, with the chain's new brand platform, "Keep On," intended to connect more emotionally with Dunkin Donuts' consumers.

BRAND VALUES

Dunkin' Donuts has a guest-first culture that results in an intense, day-in and day-out focus on keeping guests happily "running on Dunkin'." The company strives to go above and beyond people's expectations of a traditional quick-service restaurant and works to deliver best-in-class items, what the company calls "Quick Quality."

Dunkin' is also dedicated to giving back to the communities it serves, both through the generous support of its franchisees and through its Dunkin' Donuts & Baskin-Robbins Community Foundation (DDBRCF). The DDBRCF funds nonprofit organizations dedicated to providing food for the hungry, safety, and children's health. The DDBRCF has donated more than $8 million in grants to local charities. In 2014 the DDBRCF announced its largest gift in its history: a $1 million, three-year grant to Feeding America that will help support critical Feeding America initiatives nationwide, including the BackPack Program and the School Pantry Program.

FedEx ®

THE MARKET

In 1973 Yale University graduate Frederick W. Smith founded Federal Express, an airline designed to improve the speed and efficiency of overnight airfreight delivery. Its first night in operation, Federal Express delivered 186 packages to 25 cities using a fleet of 14 small aircraft. This marked the creation of a new market, providing customers access to next-business-day delivery services. Now, almost 45 years later, FedEx remains true to its original vision and purpose, helping more people and businesses around the world connect with the global marketplace.

In 1978 Fred Smith was famously quoted as saying, "The information about the package is just as important as the package itself." Since then, FedEx has been providing customers access

to timely and accurate information, enabling new supply chain models and efficiencies. This unprecedented access to information connects customers around the world to economic markets and communities.

Today, FedEx handles 12 million shipments daily, connecting more than 220 countries and territories in responsible and resourceful ways.

Smith credits the company's more than 400,000 team members around the globe with much of its success. According to Smith, "In a truly global economy, prosperity depends on global connections. Our team members make those connections happen reliably, millions of times every day."

ACHIEVEMENTS

FedEx was the first company dedicated to express package delivery and the first to offer a money-back guarantee. In 1983 FedEx was the first U.S. company to reach $1 billion in revenue without mergers and acquisitions; in 1990 FedEx became the first to win the Malcolm Baldrige National Quality Award in the services category.

The company's culture has gained wide recognition and admiration. In 2016 FedEx continued a long tradition of being named one of the most

admired and best companies to work for in the world, and one of the world's 25-best multinational workplaces as well.

HISTORY

What began in 1973 as a U.S. overnight shipping business in Memphis, Tennessee, has since expanded into a global logistics powerhouse.

Based on his unique "hub and spoke" concept developed for an economics paper written while he was a student at Yale, Smith believed that shipping items to a single, central location for mass distribution would be more efficient than shipping each item point-to-point. Today, the company is recognized as a critical player in the global economy, connecting markets that make up more than 99 percent of the world's gross domestic product.

THE PRODUCT

FedEx is a worldwide network of companies offering flexible, specialized services that represent a broad portfolio of supply chain, shipping, ecommerce, business, and related information services. The eight FedEx operating companies are FedEx Express, FedEx Ground, FedEx Freight, FedEx Office, FedEx Custom Critical, FedEx Trade Networks, FedEx SupplyChain, and FedEx CrossBorder.

RECENT DEVELOPMENTS

With annual revenues of $50.4 billion (FY2016), FedEx fosters a culture of innovation, regularly developing new solutions and technologies across its portfolio of products. Some examples follow:

GREEN FOCUS

FedEx is deeply committed to finding innovative solutions to minimize its carbon footprint and positively impact the global communities it serves. This commitment, called EarthSmart®, is designed to encourage innovation that makes the company's business — the way it works and the services it offers — more sustainable socially, economically, and environmentally. EarthSmart encourages sustainable workplace practices and opportunities for team members to engage in community outreach efforts, all for a more sustainable world.

FedEx awards the EarthSmart designation only to programs, services, and physical assets

that go beyond standard industry practices to demonstrate clear and tangible benefits to the environment, customers, team members, and local communities.

EarthSmart is not just one program but a host of initiatives that have already made

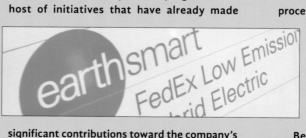

significant contributions toward the company's key sustainability benchmarks, such as reducing emissions, increasing fuel efficiency, and exceeding renewable energy goals.

EarthSmart innovations meet strict, quantifiable environmental standards. These innovations include vehicles, facilities, and customer-facing advances such as FedEx carbon-neutral envelope shipping and FedEx paperless processing.

Through EarthSmart @ Work, FedEx encourages its 400,000-plus team members to look for ways to save resources and do business more efficiently. Team members drive ideas to maximize recycling, reduce fuel emissions, and conserve energy.

Beyond business applications, FedEx has invested substantial philanthropic dollars and volunteer hours in local communities around the globe through EarthSmart Outreach. The

- FedEx Office announced in August 2016 the expansion of its managed parcel and print services designed to serve the unique shipping and printing needs of university communities. FedEx Office has designed a kit of solutions that are flexible and scalable, allowing each university to implement services on campus that meet their specific needs while creating an adaptable cost model that helps save time, labor, and overhead by freeing up resources and avoiding fixed costs associated with large-scale printing and increasing e-commerce parcel volumes.

- In July 2016 FedEx Freight launched the FedEx Freight® box in the United States. This new flat-rate freight box option makes transporting less-than-truckload (LTL) shipments simple, with improved flexibility, increased security, and — best of all — no freight classification. The FedEx Freight box packaging is included in the flat-rate cost and comes in two sizes: a standard-size freight box that requires a pallet to ship, and a smaller freight box with an integrated pallet. The freedom to choose the freight box makes freight shipping accessible for businesses, no matter the size.

FedEx sees innovation as a strategic business practice that is continuously enhanced, developed, and encouraged, whether through web services, alternative energy practices, or developing new technology and solutions.

company's outreach efforts are focused on fostering sustainable transportation, cities, and ecosystems. EarthSmart Outreach programs make measurable progress toward FedEx environmental commitments by mobilizing communities and team members to drive carbon reductions and other targeted sustainable improvements.

Whether through large-scale innovations, team member-driven initiatives, or global community service efforts, FedEx environmental contributions underscore the company's commitment to pioneering new methods to connect the world in responsible and resourceful ways. Learn more about FedEx solutions for a more sustainable world at earthsmart.fedex.com.

PROMOTION

FedEx is known for its award-winning advertising and prestigious sports sponsorships.

When it comes to advertising, FedEx brand campaigns often tout business solutions. From basic shipping and printing to full-service, strategic supply-side management, FedEx has the resources and the scale to help businesses meet their goals. FedEx's 21st-century ad campaigns include "The World On Time" (2001–present), "We Understand" (2009–present), and "We Live To Deliver" (2009–present).

Because FedEx has a lot in common with championship-caliber sports — speed, teamwork, and precision — that connection is reflected in its sports sponsorships, from FedExCup® to FedEx Racing®.

BRAND VALUES

FedEx believes that its impact is greater than the services it provides. FedEx is committed to

being a great place to work, a thoughtful steward of the environment, and a caring citizen in the communities it serves. The company is recognized as a leader in sustainability, a critical player in the global economy, and a catalyst for connecting people and places. The brand is built on firmly held beliefs.

Connected. FedEx competes collectively, connecting its brand, cultures, and successes through a global network of people, systems, and technologies. The company is constantly interacting with customers, team members, and communities to identify and connect new markets, new geographies, and new ways of doing business.

Dynamic. Team members' diverse backgrounds, talents, and perspectives drive FedEx. The company never rests — delivering daily what matters most to its customers, communities, and team. The world is always evolving, so the company never stands still or rests on its laurels.

Committed. FedEx believes it should be judged by the promises it keeps. The company is committed to making every FedEx experience outstanding, doing whatever it takes to get the job done, and finding solutions for a more sustainable world.

Innovative. FedEx champions new ways of doing business to ensure success. Never content with the status quo, team members challenge convention, push themselves, and redefine what's possible.

Excelling. FedEx raises the bar daily. The company believes that it wins when its customers win. Its team members are passionate about leading the industry and strive to exceed the expectations of customers, shareholders, and even themselves.

THINGS YOU DIDN'T KNOW ABOUT FEDEX

- ◯ The company website, fedex.com, averages more than 50 million unique visitors monthly and more than 50 million package tracking requests daily.

- ◯ The FedEx family of companies has more than 100,000 motorized vehicles for express, ground, freight, and expedited delivery service.

- ◯ All FedEx planes are named for a child of a team member.

- ◯ The Memphis World Hub has 42 miles of conveyor belts and a sorting capacity of 160,000 packages per hour and 265,000 documents per hour.

- ◯ FedEx helped engineer the first hybrid trucks.

- ◯ The majority of FedEx packaging is both recyclable and contains recycled material.

- ◯ Since 2005 the company has held FedEx Cares Week, a global week of service. More than 10,000 FedEx team members from around the world volunteered nearly 55,000 hours during this week in 2015. The tradition has expanded to nearly 500 global communities where its team members live and work.

- ◯ As part of the Trees for Troops program, FedEx donated more than 18,000 Christmas trees to military bases across the nation in 2015 alone.

- ◯ FedEx has long-term relationships with the American Red Cross, the Salvation Army, Heart to Heart International, Direct Relief International, and other organizations, bringing much-needed medicine, cots, comfort kits, water, and food supplies to affected areas immediately following natural disasters.

- ◯ FedEx is working toward a goal of using 30 percent alternative fuel in its aircraft by 2030.

THE MARKET

The pet supplies market in the United States is over $14 billion and growing every day, which is not surprising when you consider that 65 percent of US households have at least one pet in their home. In fact, today there are almost 180 million household pets in this country, which doesn't count the millions of fish, frogs, turtles, and other reptiles. And today's pets are not what they once were, rising in status to become true family members.

It's hard to think of another company as synonymous with pet supplies as the Hartz Mountain Corporation. For 90 years, anyone who has ever had a family member with fur, feathers, or scales is likely to have used a Hartz® product. Whether it was the bright orange packs of bird seed of the 1940s and 1950s, the original flea and tick collars of the 1960s and 1970s, the ever-present hamburger squeak toys, the can of Wardley® Goldfish flakes, or some of its latest innovations, Hartz has been the iconic brand of pet supply products for generations of pet-loving households. Over 25 million pet-owning households annually buy a Hartz product for their loved ones. No other pet supply company can make that claim.

ACHIEVEMENTS

Hartz has been able to secure and extend its leadership position in core categories — the ones that made the brand famous — while successfully branching into new segments. The Hartz flea and tick collar, launched in the 1960s, is the number-one flea and tick collar in the United States to this day, and Hartz flea and tick topicals for dogs are currently number one in food, drug, and mass retail.*

In a Hartz survey, vets considered Hartz's Ultraguard Pro® topical drops with the Pro-Glide™ angled applicator the easiest to use, as it glides quickly through the coat and applies smoothly on the dog's skin.

Hartz leveraged its success in the pet supplies aisle to move into the grocery aisle with biscuits and treats, introducing Hartz Crunch 'n Clean®, an innovative line of biscuits and cat

treats that combines proven dental benefits with superior taste. It was the most successful biscuit introduction of the last decade.

And although Hartz is a more recent entrant in the training pad category, Hartz Training Academy® pads quickly unseated the market leader, and Hartz pads remain the number-one training pad in the United States and Canada.

As consumers and pet parents faced the Great Recession of 2009, many shelters dealt with trying to care for more pets with less funding. Hartz donated over $3.5 million in cash and supplies in an attempt to help fill this void. More than 125 shelters throughout the United States and Canada

received support from Hartz in 2009 and 2010.

HISTORY

Hartz is an American entrepreneurial success story. In 1926 an almost penniless 26-year-old Max Stern decided to leave his native Germany for the promise of America. Germany was still suffering from the ravages of the First World War. The allure of America's stability, freedom, and economic opportunity beckoned.

A childhood friend of Stern's, a local pet dealer, had borrowed a modest sum and could only pay back the loan with 5,000 singing canaries. Stern accepted the canaries and decided to sell them in New York City. He sold the singing canaries to the John Wanamaker Department Store at Astor Place in Manhattan and soon thereafter established his business nearby at 36 Cooper Square.

Stern went back to his native Germany again and again, returning to America each time with more singing canaries that he began to sell to a growing customer base, including R. H. Macy, Sears Roebuck, F. W. Woolworth, W. T. Grant, S. S. Kresge, and others. By 1932 Stern was the largest livestock importer in America and decided to expand into packaged bird food. The Hartz Mountain line of pet products was born.

Stern's son joined the company in 1959 and expanded Hartz's product lines into goldfish, tropical fish, and a full line of aquatic supplies. Hartz expanded again in the sixties with dog and cat products, most notably the Hartz flea and tick collar — still the number-one-selling flea and tick collar for both cats and dogs.

By the early 1980s Hartz products were sold in more than 40,000 US and Canadian retail outlets. Hartz continued to expand product lines in the 1990s with the acquisition of the esteemed Wardley® brand of fish food and supplies. The portfolio also grew with the addition of the LM Animal Farms™ brand. Research facilities continued their growth as well, and new generations of pet care products were introduced under the Hartz brand, such as UltraGuard® Flea & Tick products.

In 2000 J. W. Childs Associates, LP, a leading private equity investment firm, purchased the Hartz Mountain Corporation, giving a renewed focus to research and development. The result was a collection of innovative products, such as Dentist's Best® dog chews. Sumitomo, one of the world's leading integrated global trading firms — with trade, distribution, and diversified industrial and consumer goods — acquired Hartz in 2004.

THE PRODUCT

Today Hartz is over 1,500 products strong, and it's hard to think of a type of pet whose healthy and happy life the brand isn't devoted to: dogs, cats, parakeets, canaries, parrots, cockatiels, finches, goldfish, tropical fish, reptiles, ferrets, chinchillas, guinea pigs, hamsters, and rabbits. Hartz has never lost its fundamental love of pets, which has guided the brand's expansion and focus.

RECENT DEVELOPMENTS

Hartz is full of ideas for new pet products: from advanced flea and tick protection and emerging wellness science to imaginative toys. The company consistently strives to offer exciting new ways for your pet to stay happy, healthy, and thriving.

Hartz Crunch 'n Clean biscuits are not only better for dogs' teeth, they taste great. This innovative line of biscuits and cat treats contains DentaShield®, a patented technology developed at the Indiana University School of Dentistry by a team of researchers led by Dr. George Stookey, a pioneer in fluoride research and preventative dentistry for animals and humans. Only Hartz Crunch 'n Clean biscuits and cat treats have DentaShield, which is clinically proven to reduce tartar formation for cleaner teeth. DentaShield makes Hartz biscuits and treats a more effective

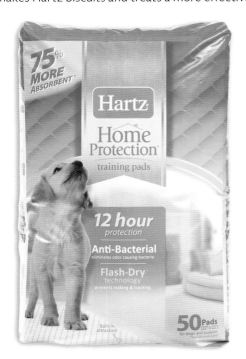

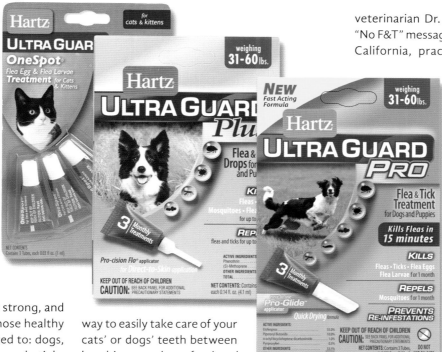

way to easily take care of your cats' or dogs' teeth between brushings and professional cleanings. Subsequently Hartz took its successful Crunch 'n Clean biscuit line one step further and extended it to Mini-Bites treats for smaller dogs.

As dental disease affects up to 80 percent of pets over the age of three, Hartz's focus on dental health does not stop with Crunch 'n Clean. The Hartz Chew 'n Clean® dog toy line offers a range of toys that satisfy the chewing needs of most dogs. The Dental Duo™ line combines a hard nylon shell with a tasty bacon-flavored center that includes the same great DentaShield ingredient to block tartar formation.

Hartz has an innovative toy line called Duraplay®. Not your average latex toy, these fun shapes have a foam-filled core for an unmatched chewing experience, and they come in colors that dogs can actually see. Chewing is only part of the playtime fun as the company also markets the Hartz Tuff Stuff® line of toss-and-retrieve toys designed with ballistic nylon to withstand that tugger in the family who always puts up a fight.

Among the newest Hartz products are Hartz® Fresh Scent™ Deodorizing Litter Beads, which add a boost of fresh scent when sprinkled onto any cat litter. The beads provide continuous freshness beyond the litter box, eliminate odors, and leave no dust or mess.

Hartz historically had only sold products and services in the United States and Canada. Since joining the Sumitomo family, Hartz is now sold in over 50 countries around the world, including Russia, the United Kingdom, Mexico, and Japan.

PROMOTION

Year-round flea and tick protection is vital to your pet's health. That's why Hartz is committed to providing vet-quality flea and tick protection at half the price. Hartz has campaigned to educate consumers and vets alike that paying higher prices for flea and tick treatments does not guarantee better flea and tick protection. Renowned

veterinarian Dr. Bernadine Cruz promotes the "No F&T" messaging through her Laguna Woods, California, practice, as well as through her Internet-based radio show, The Pet Doctor, heard on PetLifeRadio.com.

Hartz also supports the America Veterinary Medical Association's annual Pet Dental Health month each February to get the word out to pet parents about proper dental care.

Hartz is very active in the pet and human communities alike. For example, Hartz sent a team to the Strut Your Mutt walkathon to raise funds for the Best Friends Animal Society. Hartz is also a supporter of the Wounded Warrior Project (WWP), which provides programs and services to wounded veterans. The company donates a percentage of sales at military stores to the WWP.

BRAND VALUES

Hartz understands that the relationship you have with your pet is unique and special, and Hartz honors that relationship every day, in everything the company does. The pet people at Hartz don't just strive to understand the human-animal bond, they live it. Hartz offers the finest-quality pet supplies to help your pet live a healthier, happier, and longer life. The brand is solely focused on delivering for consumers exceptional pet care products that are held to the strictest standards of leading regulatory bodies, such as the US Environmental Protection Agency and Food and Drug Administration. Hartz works with a network of internal and external pet experts to deliver products designed to help pet parents provide top-quality pet care. Hartz's love of pets is reflected in its entire line of products.

* Excluding Walmart.

IZOD

THE MARKET

The IZOD brand is a youthful, energetic, sports-inspired, global brand. Since its introduction in the United States 80-plus years ago, IZOD has evolved into an American institution and a sportswear authority. Having had multiple sponsorships in professional golf, car racing, football, and basketball, the brand has continued to keep visibility up among sports fans of all ages.

ACHIEVEMENTS

IZOD has a defined presence in the golf arena and has been linked to sports since sports moved firmly into the field of commerce. A number of promotional partnerships — including sponsorships with PGA players Webb Simpson, Scott Piercy, Spencer Levin, and Cameron Wilson, and AAU Boys Basketball — have continued the athletic-inspired direction of the apparel's brand.

The brand's first-known connection in sports was the 1932 Olympia International Horse Show,

where A. J. Izod presented the Dozi Championship Cup ("Dozi" is Izod spelled backward). Walter Hagen, a major figure in golf in the first half of the 20th century and the first native-born American to win the British Open, is quoted in *The Professional Golfers' Association Tour: A History* as saying, "I traveled first class, and that included a suite at the Savoy at five pounds at day, the Chez

Paris, cocktail hour at the Ritz, the Daimler car with chauffeur and footman, fine silk shirts custom tailored by A. J. Izod on Conduit Street just off the Strand."

Vincent Draddy of the David Crystal Company was also pivotal in introducing the Izod shirt to American golfers. Draddy, an avid golfer, was able to introduce the Izod shirts to his famous friends Ben Hogan, Sam Snead, and others. Then the business's visibility boomed, and the Izod brand and its sports apparel soon became regularly featured in *Gentry Magazine*. Since being brought under the PVH umbrella, IZOD has continued its sports legacy. In the 1990s IZOD became the official sponsor of the Ladies Professional Golf Association (LPGA). The original Brendan Byrne Arena at the Meadowlands in New Jersey was branded the IZOD Center in a 2007 deal that reflected the brand's sportslike DNA. That original agreement was extended until the state of New Jersey decided to close the center.

In 2009 IZOD became the official apparel provider of the Indy Racing League, Indy Car Series, Firestone Indy Light Series, and the Indianapolis

Motor Speedway. In 2010 Izod added the official title sponsorship of the Indy Car Series, aligning its athletically inspired product and target audience with a national pastime.

Additionally, IZOD made its mark on the art and photography world. One of the brand's first

American editorial features was in the July 5, 1930, *Vogue,* a sports issue. The world-renowned George Hoyningen-Heuene photograph titled *Bathing Suits: A. J. Izod, Ltd., London* featured a two-piece IZOD swimming suit with garnet-red trunks and a mixed red-and-white top of machine-knit alpaca wool.

HISTORY

IZOD's roots go back to Arthur James "Jack" Izod's bespoke tailor shop in London, where Jack Izod produced shirts and held a royal warrant to provide them to the royal household. A visiting executive from David Crystal Inc. became intrigued by the name and purchased the rights to it. The Izod of London mark was initially applied to a successful line of women's shirts and then expanded to include menswear and childrenswear. David Crystal Inc. first added color to the line and subsequently coupled the brand with the Lacoste brand in order to broaden selection and appeal. IZOD's athletic roots and colorful persona were thus first formed. Now associated with the legendary French tennis player René Lacoste but still lagging in sales, the David Crystal Inc. executive began giving away the shirts to famous people, including the Duke of Windsor, Sam Snead, Ben Hogan, and Bing Crosby; the shirts started resonating with consumers.

Over time, the shirts became popularized as IZOD shirts, and by the 1980s they had become a signature piece of preppy wardrobes in the United States. When the preppy look began to

fade at the end of the decade, so did the brand's sales. IZOD's owner, at this point known as Crystal Brands, split the IZOD and Lacoste brands in the early 1990s in an effort to maintain market share, marketing similarly designed goods at different price points and in different channels but without success. Lacoste was sold, and PVH purchased IZOD in 1995.

Continuing IZOD's association with sports, the brand signed multiyear sponsorship deals with golfers Webb Simpson, Scott Piercy, and Spencer Levin in 2012, the three IZOD brand ambassadors forming "Team IZOD." Cameron Wilson joined that team in 2014.

THE PRODUCT

IZOD products cover a range of classic athletically inspired sportswear, golfwear, jeanswear, performance wear, accessories, and luxury-style sport collections. The IZOD brand continues to grow as well, and has been licensed for additional product categories, including leather outerwear and watches.

RECENT DEVELOPMENTS

The brand has continued to expand internationally. In 2011 PVH announced a strategic licensing arrangement with a Chinese partner, which committed to distribute IZOD-branded men's sportswear in more than 1,000 points of sale across China, one of the world's fastest-growing markets. The brand is also licensed to a major apparel company in India for men's sportswear and accessories, another emerging economy with significant potential.

PVH in 2015 closed IZOD's retail business to focus on the growing IZOD wholesale market, and the year also saw launch of the IZOD Tour+ golf apparel line. IZOD brand ambassador and 2012 US Open champion Webb Simpson debuted the line at the 2015 Masters Tournament, which was first made available to consumers exclusively at select Dick's Sporting Goods and Golf Galaxy stores.

Eyewear provider ClearVision Optical introduced IZOD Interchangeable eyewear in 2016, a new collection that lets consumers customize their eyewear by changing the temple color to match their look.

PROMOTION

IZOD's products can be found in department store shop-in-shops, licensed retail stores, and specialty retail stores. Point-of-sale displays reflect the brand's aesthetic as an outdoors, sporty, and youthful American brand. IZOD promotes its products through point-of-sale displays, television, print advertisements, fixture design, social media sites, and sponsorships.

While continuing to elevate IZOD's fashion, quality, and design, PVH has also focused on growing the brand's department store presence and profitability. The company has invested in in-store branding, such as installing new shop-in-shops in mid-tier department stores. These shops feature the best and most expansive department store presentation of the IZOD brand — colorful, performance-oriented, and inspired by an active lifestyle. Last, given the heightened focus on golf and the brand's objective to increase the size of its golf business, IZOD continues to look for new, brand-appropriate ways to touch a broader audience.

BRAND VALUES

Today's IZOD collections remain true to the brand's history of colorful style and functional design. IZOD's products evolve with customer needs while adhering to the brand's youthful and active persona, thereby enabling IZOD to become one of the most popular sportswear brands in the United States.

THINGS YOU DIDN'T KNOW ABOUT IZOD

○ **The interlocking IZ logo was introduced in 2003.**

○ **The first IZOD shop opened on 49 Conduit Street in London's famed West End.**

○ **Former president Dwight D. Eisenhower wore IZOD while playing golf in the 1960s.**

KONICA MINOLTA

THE MARKET

Corporations, health-care facilities, legal providers, and educational systems are all adopting new and more cost-effective strategies for handling documents, distributing information, and accessing the essential data to accomplish their missions. Portable and mobile devices are overcoming the problems of distance and time, keeping headquarters and branch locations in close touch with managers and practitioners on the go. Advanced security systems are protecting personal data more effectively to comply with increasingly complex regulations. Environmental concerns are driving the search for energy-saving strategies and waste-reduction programs that protect the planet for generations to come.

Linking all these emerging business and professional trends is the need for a central information resource that can interface seamlessly with industry-standard software solutions. Konica Minolta has led the way with built-in scanning to multiple destinations, improving

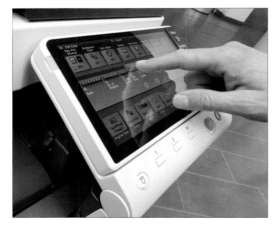

efficiency by digitizing, distributing, and managing information more quickly and cost-effectively. Konica Minolta has also developed document and IT strategies focused specifically on the needs of professional as well as general business applications — serving corporate and vertical-market end-users with specialized workflows and processes that allow hardware and software to work together with greater speed, simplicity, and security.

ACHIEVEMENTS

Konica Minolta's strategy is paying real dividends in customer satisfaction. For the ninth straight year — in 2016 — Konica Minolta has been named the number-one brand for customer loyalty in the MFP Office Product Copier Category in an independent survey conducted by Brand Keys. This honor recognizes the company's strong and continuing relationships with its U.S. installed customer base. The Konica Minolta business solutions group also earned the Line of the Year award from BLI in 2014, as well as multiple citations from BERTL Inc. BLI has honored Konica Minolta with its Outstanding Achievement Award for Energy Efficiency, and Konica Minolta has repeatedly been named to the Dow Jones Sustainability World Index in recognition of the company's economic, environmental, and social performance.

Konica Minolta's All Covered IT Services division, the delivery vehicle for helping customers manage their printing, document workflow, infrastructure, and security needs without adding personnel to their payroll, has been named as one of the top ten Managed IT service providers for the fifth consecutive year by MSPmentor 501, a distinguished list and report identifying the world's top 501 Managed Service Providers (MSPs). Konica Minolta environmental

efforts have also led to product certification according to strict industry standards, including Energy Star, Eco-Mark, Blue Angel, and other worldwide programs.

HISTORY

Konica and Minolta merged their business operations in 2003, refocusing their efforts on business and professional products and software and increasing their cutting-edge research programs in digital and optical technology. Konica's history goes back to 1873, when founder Rokusaburo Sagiura began selling photographic materials at his Tokyo apothecary; in 1971 Konica released Japan's first plain-paper photocopier. Minolta was founded in 1928 as a camera manufacturer; its innovations include the world's first magnification and reduction photocopier and the world's first photocopier to produce two-color images in a single pass.

Today, Konica Minolta has over 41,600 employees worldwide, more than 20 top-ranked manufacturing facilities, and offices in 50 countries on six continents. In the United States,

EnvisionIT

NEW WAYS TO WORK FASTER AND SMARTER.

Konica Minolta is a world leader in green initiatives that protect the planet for future generations. In manufacturing, Konica Minolta has pioneered programs that reduce greenhouse gases, minimize pollution, eliminate hazardous substances, and develop safe alternatives to toxic chemicals. Konica Minolta's exclusive Simitri® polymerized toner also leads the way in using plant-based biomass materials that make it more friendly to the environment, reducing CO_2 emissions and cutting toner consumption by more than 30 percent. Also unique to Konica Minolta is a type of recycled plastic used in the company's devices. Polyethylene Terephthalate, or PET, the substance that makes up most recycled bottles, lacks the stiffness required for use in printer products. To use PET as a printer component, it must be mixed with fiberglass or carbon fiber, making it difficult to recycle. Konica Minolta's chemists have developed a unique process to blend recycled PET with polycarbonate in order to achieve the stiffness required for its products without sacrificing ease of recycling.

Konica Minolta Business Solutions U.S.A. Inc. is an industry leader in advanced document management technologies and IT Services, with complete business solutions incorporating multifunctional peripherals (MFPs), production print systems, digital presses, and related services and supplies. The company is headquartered in New Jersey and provides world-class sales and service through a network of 115 direct sales locations and roughly 350 dealer partners.

COUNT ON
KONICA MINOLTA

THE PRODUCT

Konica Minolta's product line covers document needs from desktop to print shop. The company's bizhub digital MFPs provide superior color and black-and-white image quality, high-speed output, proven reliability, and modular design. Konica Minolta bizhub PRO and bizhub PRESS equipment continues to set the pace in digital production print applications, helping lead the transition to digital print systems that offer superior color reproduction, variable data capabilities, and simple setup procedures to reduce labor costs and make short-run printing more affordable. A broad range of network-ready desktop printers and printer/copiers help corporate and professional customers create right-size fleets that save energy by reducing the need for underutilized or redundant devices.

RECENT DEVELOPMENTS

Konica Minolta's latest line of bizhub color and black-and-white MFPs provide end-users with a significant innovation: the familiar touch-screen interface of tablet PCs. Users can touch and swipe, drag and drop, pinch-in/pinch-out, toggle, and perform other control steps more quickly and intuitively, making operation simple even for first-time or temporary personnel.

At the heart of bizhub performance are technology innovations based upon Konica Minolta's bizhub OP (Open Platform) system, their award-winning Emperon® Print System, and bEST (bizhub Extended Solution Technology) design that allows for third-party software control directly on the bizhub screen. Konica Minolta also continues to innovate in service and support. The company's All Covered IT Services are especially valuable in helping clients migrate to cloud services that save time and money as well as protect and secure valuable data. Other programs such as Optimized Print Services use advanced metrics to analyze current print practices and create energy and cost savings by redeploying devices more efficiently and modifying employee behavior to minimize unnecessary printing.

At the high end of production print performance, the bizhub PRESS C8000 color printer incorporates innovative technology for maintaining color quality and stability through long press runs, even at a high-speed output of 80 pages per minute.

In 2014 Konica-Minolta became a distributor for 3D Systems' 3D printers, making it the first OEM to sell, support, and service 3D printers through the traditional U.S. printer and office equipment channel.

In 2016 the company acquired Meridian Imaging Solutions, a managed print and IT services firm, in an effort to expand its footprint in the nation's capital. The acquisition aligns with Konica Minolta's desire to provide a full range of services for the workplace.

PROMOTION

Konica Minolta Business Solutions launched a national advertising campaign in 2014 in support of its bizhub brand. The campaign utilized a highly integrated mix of media designed to communicate Konica Minolta's new approach to business and its new bizhub brand, including national network and cable television, print advertising, direct mail, online initiatives and outdoor/ stadium advertising to maximize impact and reach targeted audiences across the United States. The Konica Minolta advertising efforts were supported by the "What If" global advertising campaign.

In a 2016 Konica Minolta Business Solutions TV spot, a dapper spokesperson walks through the Konica Minolta headquarters. These employees, he says, take pride in that the people they serve don't care what they do — they allow customers to focus on their own business. He explains how the people of Konica Minolta provide secure cloud service (as he walks into a literal cloud), expert IT support (he crowd surfs through the IT staff), innovative technology like medical imaging (the viewers now see him as a skeleton), and a whole host of printing capabilities (as he prints a 3-D photo of his face). With everything Konica Minolta does, customers can attend to what they do best.

Continuing to expand its brand within the golf community, Konica Minolta announced in 2016 a multiyear partnership with rising golf phenomenon and winner of the 2016 Fred Haskins award as the nation's top collegiate golfer, Beau Hossler. As part of this partnership, Hossler has agreed to serve as a global ambassador for the company and participate in their marketing and various social media campaigns. The deal also calls for Hossler to wear the Konica Minolta logo on the sleeve of his apparel and participate in customer entertainment at select events around the country.

BRAND VALUES

The vision of Konica Minolta has been consistent throughout a long history of successful growth: to be a trusted, reliable partner that delivers long-term value and utilizes a diverse and engaged workforce to produce consistent benefits for customers and stakeholders.

Throughout the world, Konica Minolta works to be a responsible global citizen — respecting laws, protecting the environment, preventing pollution, and continually pursuing initiatives to counter climate change. Konica Minolta focuses on the customer experience to develop industry-leading document solutions, leverage expertise in vertical markets, promote the benefits of technological education, and invest in best-in-class business practices to boost productivity — today, tomorrow, and for years to come.

THINGS YOU DIDN'T KNOW ABOUT KONICA MINOLTA

- ○ Konica marketed Japan's first brand-name camera in 1903.

- ○ A specially modified Minolta camera was carried aboard the spacecraft Friendship 7 on John Glenn's historic orbital flight.

- ○ Konica Minolta is starting production of OLED (Organic Light Emitting Diode) Lighting Panels — the world's most power-efficient design.

LAND O'LAKES, INC.

THE MARKET

While Land O'Lakes might be best known for its flagship butter business, the company offers an extensive line of dairy-based consumer, foodservice, and food ingredients products, and holds the number-one U.S. market position in the butter, deli cheese, and branded dairy-based foodservice markets.

Land O'Lakes' MoArk, LLC, subsidiary is the nation's second-largest marketer of shell eggs and the top marketer of branded and specialty eggs.

Land O'Lakes also is a leading supplier of agricultural inputs and services — giving the company a farm-to-fork presence in the agricultural and food marketplace.

Land O'Lakes Purina Feed is the nation's number-one marketer of livestock and lifestyle animal feeds, under the Purina® and LAND O LAKES® Feed brands.

Winfield Solutions, LLC, distributes the popular CROPLAN GENETICS® seed and AgriSolutions™ crop protection product brands, which have helped establish Land O'Lakes as the nation's top seed and crop protection products wholesaler.

ACHIEVEMENTS

Throughout its 90-plus-year history, Land O'Lakes has been known for being the gold standard in butter. The company's flagship butter and the familiar Indian Maiden logo are icons of a diverse dairy foods product line.

Market- and consumer-focused innovation are hallmarks of Land O'Lakes' dairy foods products, with research and development experts and a test kitchen staff turning out innovative products and industry firsts — like the first no-fat sour cream, Spreadable Butter with Canola Oil, and FlavorProtect® packaging, which keeps products tasting fresh.

This focus on innovation also is a driver at the LongView Animal Nutrition Center, a research facility that develops a wide range of animal nutrition products and holds more than 80 patents for feed products and manufacturing

processes. Breakthroughs include the first-ever young animal (calf) milk replacers, "senior" horse feeds, and weather-resistant feed technologies.

In the crop inputs businesses, the company consistently delivers new seed genetics and traits, as well as innovative crop protection products. At more than 200 Answer Plot® demonstration locations across the United States, the company gives farmers a firsthand look at how technologies, products, and production practices perform in the field.

Land O'Lakes also has been recognized for its efforts to promote global food security, which is achieved through the development and delivery of products and services that enhance agricultural productivity and sustainability, as well as through the company's involvement with international development and humanitarian projects. From 2010 to 2014, Land O'Lakes International Development managed 31 agriculture and enterprise development projects in 21 countries, which were funded primarily by the U.S. Department of Agriculture (USDA), the United States Agency for International Development (USAID), and USAID's Office of Foreign Disaster Assistance (OFDA). These projects were implemented in Africa, Asia, and the Middle East through partnerships that generate economic growth, improve health and nutrition, and alleviate poverty.

HISTORY

Land O'Lakes' history began in 1921, when 300 Minnesota-based, farmer-owned cooperative creameries joined together to form the Minnesota Cooperative Creameries Association — a butter marketing cooperative.

The goal was to capture value from the marketplace for members by enhancing product quality, brand strength, and consumer-focused innovation. By 1926 the association's LAND O LAKES–branded butter was so popular that the company changed its name to Land O'Lakes Creameries Inc. — which later became Land O'Lakes Inc.

In 1929, the year the Depression-era economy began taking its toll, the cooperative took another step to serve members by entering the farm inputs business. The new Agricultural Services Division — with feed, seed, and equipment operations — ensured a reliable, competitively priced, high-quality supply of products for members. As the ag services business grew, the same innovation and brand strength that were the foundation of the dairy foods business became hallmarks of the ag services operations.

The next three decades saw continued growth, as Land O'Lakes moved aggressively into the cheese business, established a position as the leading U.S. manufacturer of dry milk products, expanded its ag inputs business, and opened its first research farm, where new animal feeds, seeds, and fertilizers were developed and tested.

A variety of mergers and acquisitions continued the cooperative's strategic growth through the 1960s, '70s, and '80s. During this time, Land O'Lakes also expanded its research and development capabilities, both in the test kitchens and by opening the Land O'Lakes Answer Farm (1974), an agricultural research center.

Growth continued through the 1990s, as a coast-to-coast dairy procurement and processing system was developed to support national brand and marketing efforts. A key development in the ag inputs business was the launch of the first-ever Answer Plot®, a unique, in-the-country program for developing and sharing crop production products, insights, and techniques. Answer Plot® sites have now expanded beyond the United States to several international locations.

As Land O'Lakes entered the 21st century, strategic growth continued, including the acquisition of Purina Mills (feed) in 2001, which brought the iconic Purina checkerboard to Land O'Lakes. In 2007, Land O'Lakes consolidated its seed and crop protection products businesses under the WinField™ Solutions banner — creating a dynamic business that is pursuing rapid growth.

Today, Land O'Lakes continues to be a member-owned cooperative. It is the nation's second-largest cooperative and number 215 on the Fortune 500 list. The company does business in all 50 states and more than 50 countries, with the distinction of being the leading marketer of a full line of dairy-based consumer, foodservice, and food ingredient products in the United States; serving international customers with food and animal feed ingredients; and providing producers with an extensive line of agricultural supplies and services.

THE PRODUCT

Land O'Lakes' line of dairy products starts with the flagship branded butter and extends to more than a dozen branded butter products, including Light Butter, Whipped Butter, and an innovative line of spreadable butters. Cheese offerings are also varied, with more than three dozen cheeses in the company's market-leading deli-cheese line (offered under the LAND O LAKES® and

Alpine Lace® brands). The LAND O LAKES® brand also is found on dairy-case cheese, margarines, sour cream, fluid milk, and a host of other dairy products. In addition, the company is a leader in the dairy-based foodservice and ingredients markets.

The LAND O LAKES® brand is also prominent in the egg market, led by the company's branded All-Natural, Cage-Free, Organic, and Omega-3 Eggs.

Through Land O'Lakes Purina Feed, the company serves more than 4,500 local cooperatives and independent Purina® dealers across the United States. This business offers hundreds of animal nutrition products for horses, dairy and beef cattle, goats, swine, poultry, rabbits, game animals, exotics, and many more.

Through Winfield Solutions, LLC, Land O'Lakes supports its farmer-owners and dealers with a wide range of crop inputs (seed and crop protection products), led by the CROPLAN GENETICS® seed and AgriSolutions™ crop protection products. The company delivers the latest in seed genetics and traits, as well as advanced crop protection products that enhance productivity and sustainability.

RECENT DEVELOPMENTS

Whether it's LAND O LAKES® Butter with Olive Oil and Sea Salt, EcoCare® Feeds, Brown Eggs with Omega-3, or top-quality Origin® plant nutrients, Land O'Lakes consistently delivers innovative, industry-leading products.

Land O'Lakes also continues to strengthen its links to its farmer-members, consumers, commercial customers, and key communities. With vibrant corporate and consumer websites, consumer blogs, a growing presence in social media, and a host of other communications tools, Land O'Lakes is working to maintain close relationships with its key constituents.

That's why Land O'Lakes donates 2 percent or more of its pretax profits to the Land O'Lakes Foundation. With these funds and the help of volunteer efforts, the foundation strives to fight hunger, support education, and strengthen communities. Through programs like the Member Co-op Match, Matching Gifts to Education, and annual United Way campaign, Land O'Lakes is fulfilling the foundation's mission to serve the many communities where members and employees live and work. In 2015, the foundation made more than $11 million in financial and product donations. The cooperatives' employees contributed almost 30,000 volunteer hours.

Individual businesses within Land O'Lakes also focus on community and corporate citizenship. MoArk, LLC, for example, has donated more than 1 million fresh eggs to food shelves; Winfield Solutions sponsored a series of community gardens; the dairy foods product line is part of General Mills' Box Tops for Education program; and Land O'Lakes Purina Feed's Pink 50 campaign increased awareness and funding for breast cancer research.

PROMOTION

Land O'Lakes' promotional and marketing programs focus on innovation and quality — in the products and services the company delivers and in the insights and expertise it shares with consumers and commercial customers.

Land O'Lakes dairy foods' communications center around the "Where Simple Goodness Begins™" theme — focusing on the purity and freshness of LAND O LAKES® dairy products. The company's online "Simple Rewards®" program provides special offers to consumers.

In its feed products, marketing programs concentrate on quality and the difference the "right feed" can make — whether the customer is a livestock producer, owns show animals, or just enjoys the companionship of pets. Promotions include the Better Animals® program, the Purina® 60-Day See the Difference Challenge, and the Purina® Difference™ Rewards program.

In the crop inputs area, efforts focus on translating crop production insights and expertise into competitive advantage, led by the Winfield Solutions® organization's Answer Plot® and Expert Seller programs.

BRAND VALUES

The Land O'Lakes Inc. corporate brand is built on a set of clearly articulated "Values," as follows:

People. We believe in and value people and are dedicated to a diverse and inclusive workforce and culture.

Performance. We value and reward performance and believe in setting high standards and clear goals, and encouraging and recognizing initiative that enables us to deliver on these goals.

Customer Commitment. We value customers and believe maintaining strong, responsive, and enduring customer relationships is fundamental to our success.

Quality. We value quality in all that we do and are committed to delivering the highest-quality products and services — continually making our best even better.

Integrity. We value integrity and maintain an unwavering commitment to honesty and openness.

THINGS YOU DIDN'T KNOW ABOUT LAND O'LAKES INC.

○ In 2015, through the efforts of the Land O'Lakes Foundation, more than 600,000 servings of food were grown at community gardens.

○ If Land O'Lakes' annual production of butter sticks was laid end to end, it would circle the globe 1.5 times.

○ LAND O LAKES® Butter has only two ingredients: sweet cream and salt.

○ Each day, more than 1 million horses are fed Land O'Lakes Purina Feed products.

SINCE 1868

Martinelli's

GOLD MEDAL®

"Drink Your Apple a Day"®

HISTORY

S. Martinelli & Company — Martinelli's — offers a quintessential story of family, place, connections, and commitment. Nearing its 150th anniversary in business, located in the same California valley as the day production began, and looking toward its fifth generation of family leadership, Martinelli's hit upon a formula for success, and its core principles aren't going away any time soon.

In 1859 Stephen G. Martinelli, a young Swiss immigrant, settled with his brother, Louis, in the temperate and fertile Pajaro Valley near Monterey Bay, where the apples were of exceptional quality for making cider. In 1868 he founded S. Martinelli & Company, producing bottle-fermented Champagne Cider with apples from California's first commercial orchards. In addition, they also produced soft drinks, including ginger ale and an orange "champagne," which became known as a "delicious temperance drink." The expanding business moved to its current location in the center of Watsonville in 1885. A steam-powered cider mill was constructed, new tanks and bottling equipment were installed, and a 40-acre apple orchard was planted to assure a supply of the best varieties. In 1890 Martinelli was awarded the first-prize gold medal at the California State Fair, leading to the adoption of the brand trademark, "Martinelli's Gold Medal."

Then, in the early 20th century, many cities passed laws against alcohol consumption and distribution, a precursor to Prohibition. Facing this threat to the business head-on, Stephen G.

Martinelli Jr., while a student at the University of California in 1916, developed a process for making unfermented apple juice. In the summer of 1917 the company produced the first few thousand cases of unfermented, pure apple juice, pasteurized in pint bottles. Prohibition was enacted nationwide in 1920, and the company grew by specializing in nonalcoholic apple juice products, including the first non-alcoholic sparkling cider. Thanks to the development of this unique product, Martinelli's made quite a name for itself in the 1920s. Sparkling cider became the drink of choice for the US Navy in its Hawaiian operations in 1925, and in 1929 it became the "Champagne of the movies," as filmmakers used it to replace champagne in the glasses of movie stars on the silver screen. Its popularity grew, and Martinelli's unique "Golden Apple" jug was introduced in 1933, along with the slogan, "Drink Your Apple A Day."

Today, S. Martinelli & Company is managed by the founder's grandson, Stephen C. Martinelli (chairman of the board) and great-grandson S. John Martinelli (president).

Continuing plant modernization and expansion, along with improvements in packaging and distribution, have enabled the family-owned and privately held Martinelli Company to keep pace with consumer demand for premium, 100 percent–natural apple juice products.

ACHIEVEMENTS

The essence of Martinelli's award-winning taste is found in the brand's fundamental principles: 100 percent US-grown fresh apples, not from concentrate, cold processed up to the point of pasteurization. Fresh apples of the finest varieties, including the flavorful Newtown Pippin, are blended to achieve a balance of natural sweetness and tartness. The apples are thoroughly washed and hand-sorted to remove any below-standard apples, then milled and pressed to release the fresh juice.

Martinelli's premium, 100 percent apple juices are flash-pasteurized, hot-filled into new bottles, capped, and quickly cooled to retain the natural apple flavor. Martinelli's Sparkling

Cider and other sparkling 100 percent juices are carbonated, cold-filled, capped, then slowly pasteurized and cooled in the bottle. The pasteurization process assures product purity and quality for extended shelf life without preservatives. At every step in Martinelli's Gold Medal process, the most sophisticated quality control methods are applied.

Martinelli's Gold Medal apple juice and cider (the traditional name for apple juice) are identical. Both are premium-quality 100 percent juice from US-grown fresh apples, with no concentrates, no added water, no preservatives, no sweeteners, and no additives of any kind.

Since Martinelli's first gold medal in 1890, the company has received more than 50 med-

als for product excellence at state, national, and international expositions.

Martinelli's has three facilities in Watsonville, totaling over 600,000 square feet on 40 acres, with all warehousing located in Watsonville, California. Approximately 200 people are employed from the local community.

Distribution of Martinelli's Gold Medal products now extends to every state in the United States and several other countries in North and South America, the Caribbean, Asia, and the Middle East.

LEGACY
The Martinelli family has maintained a business model for almost 150 years that has now become a byword for 21st-century economics and society: staying local.

The Martinellis are part of the Watsonville community — not just as the oldest and one of the largest employers, but as coaches and leaders in the neighborhood. Relations with growers go back generations. Their historic building has sat across the street from the Watsonville high

school since the 1800s, and has sold cases of juice and cider to members of the community and visitors right from its front doors. This location also housed a small museum that included a collection celebrating not only their own history but also the history of the Pajaro Valley. In celebration of its 150th anniversary, Martinelli's will open a visitors' center at a new location in Watsonville, and will house a new museum and store to represent their business and great community.

Apples are still grown in the Pajaro Valley. Martinelli's actually pays a higher than market value for local crop to encourage growers to keep its orchards in production. The company also buys every locally grown apple it can find because of the higher quality. Due to the Pajaro Valley's climate, Watsonville produces apples of high sugar content, especially the Newtown Pippin, allowing for what the founder described as a superior flavor of juice. Production season begins in fall, during the harvest season, and — thanks to the modern developments of cold storage — can last until early summer.

With the vast majority of its fruit grown in Pajaro Valley orchards such as Corralitos and in the nearby San Juan Bautista and Hollister areas, Martinelli's represents not just the financial

means for apple farms to survive but also a sense of pride for farmers to be associated with a company known for making quality products for more than 140 years.

LOOKING AHEAD
With its core principles firmly in place, Martinelli's has faced challenges in past decades regarding a possible need to move from its Watsonville home. However, plants acquired from Green Giant and Birdseye Frozen Food allowed Martinelli's to expand its business while remaining in the same area, without need to develop and build manufacturing facilities from scratch — an especially intensive effort when food processing is involved.

For the first time in nearly a century and a half, Martinelli's is considering purchase of a farm to grow its own apples. John Martinelli explains that his great-grandfather's brother was an apple

farmer, which was the last time anyone in the family grew apples. With its own farm, Martinelli's can plant the varieties that make its juice quality and flavor the best in the business. "We want to plant heirloom varieties that aren't popular on the fresh market due to their appearance, but make a better-tasting juice."

In keeping with tradition, and in anticipation for the future of the family business, Martinelli's is beginning to manage the shift of operations to its fifth generation.

Classic Facts and Anecdotes

- Founder Stephen G. Martinelli organized and led the Watsonville Swiss Band during the town's early years.

- The company's brand began with award-winning fermented cider, containing around 7 percent alcohol, but became famous with its production of nonalcoholic cider.

- John Martinelli personally tastes every day's production of juice to make sure it's up to standard.

- Every serving of Martinelli's juice contains two and a half apples in it.

- Martinelli's special blend of US-grown fresh apples contains a mix of more than a half-dozen apples that produce a premium flavor, including Honey Crisp, Pink Lady, Gala, Fuji, and Granny Smith, with the standout player being the Newtown Pippin. Martinelli's consistent quality comes from getting the right blend of apples each season as apple varieties and natural flavor vary from season to season, affecting their tartness and sweetness. No sugars, water, or flavors are added to enhance the natural juice, so the flavor may be slightly different from lot to lot, but the quality is always consistent.

C.F. Martin & Co.
EST. 1833

HISTORY

The guitar is the most popular musical instrument in the world today, and ever since the guitar began to take hold in the early 1800s, C. F. Martin has been inextricably intertwined in the guitar's evolution and innovation. Although economic conditions went through periods of great instability, Martin was able to survive the Civil War, the Spanish-American War, World War I, the Great Depression, World War II, and even the disco decade. The formula for Martin's success is and always has been an unparalleled commitment to precise handcraftsmanship blended with optimum tonewoods and singular design. Martin remains the oldest surviving maker of stringed instruments in the world, and the most respected maker of acoustic guitars in America.

Having studied instrument making in the shop of Viennese luthier Johann Stauffer, Christian Frederick Martin returned to his hometown of Markneukirchen in what is now eastern Germany. The town's violin makers considered the guitar little more than furniture and forbade him from practicing his trade. Although he was eventually vindicated, hurt feelings and the death of his father caused him to pack his tools and emigrate with his wife and two children to the freedom and excitement of the New World. He arrived in New York City in November 1833 and promptly set up a thriving music store near what is now the mouth of the Holland Tunnel. Unhappy in New

York, he moved his family to Nazareth, Pennsylvania, in 1839. In this small town of Germanic immigrants, his exquisitely made instruments evolved to provide the very definition of the American guitar.

For more than 183 years, Martin guitars have been prized for their tone, consistency, quality, beauty, and attention to handcrafted detail. Professional and amateur musicians in every genre of music hold Martin guitars in high esteem. Among the extensive list of famous musicians who have owned and played Martin guitars are Elvis Presley, Paul McCartney, John Lennon, Bob Dylan, Paul Simon, Eric Clapton, Joan Baez, Sting, Johnny Cash, Gene Autry, Hank Williams, Jimmy Buffett, Jimmy Page, Tom Petty, Willie Nelson, and Crosby, Stills, Nash & Young, to name just a few.

ACHIEVEMENTS

While Martin's many contributions to the evolution of the guitar are well documented, the most significant and memorable innovations include the invention of the X-bracing pattern in 1843, the invention of the Dreadnought guitar design in 1916, and the development of the 14-fret neck for acoustic guitars in 1929. Often overlooked are

the many dozens of guitar, ukulele, and mandolin shapes and sizes that Martin originated. To meet musicians' increasing need for volume, the guitar grew in size from a relatively small instrument played by women in the parlors of their homes into the larger, more resonant guitars that we know today. With each incremental increase in size, Martin captured a tremendous variety of tonal textures, giving guitarists a seemingly unending array of tonality for the varied styles and genres of their music.

The first appearance of the now-famous X-bracing pattern was seen on a Martin guitar in 1843. This ingenious bracing system provides strength for the soundboard without the use of excessive support for the top, which can inhibit a guitar's tone. X-bracing is now a standard feature on virtually all steel-string guitars worldwide.

Martin's 14-fret neck design was developed in late 1929. Prior to the period, guitars were generally equipped with a 12-fret neck. As the story goes, a renowned plectrum banjoist of the day, Perry Bechtel, suggested to Frank Henry Martin that he make a guitar with a longer neck that would allow for more access to the upper notes. Following Bechtel's advice, Martin introduced a guitar with the longer neck and dubbed it an "Orchestra Model" (OM). The 14-fret neck was so well received that Martin eventually extended the

feature to all models in its line. In short order, 14 frets became the standard design for the entire guitar industry and are acknowledged as being optimum for fingerstyle guitar technique.

The Martin Dreadnought model made its first public appearance in 1916, produced exclusively by Martin for the Oliver Ditson Company of Boston and New York. Ditson went out of business in the early 1930s, and Martin subsequently incorporated these tonally powerful models into its own

sustained and, at the same time, to see how boldly we have moved into the future."

Martin's continuing popularity is attributed to a general resurgence of acoustic guitar music, an ever-increasing respect for Martin's high level of craftsmanship, and Chris Martin's bold yet open-minded management style. In 2004 Martin completed its 1,000,000th instrument, and remarkably, just seven years later, Martin completed Serial #1,500,000, based upon Leonardo DaVinci's timeless artwork. These priceless milestone Martin guitars can be seen in Martin's beautiful Museum & Visitors Center, which was completed in 2006.

As computers and technology dominate culture, guitars have also embraced the digital world. Martin responded with an array of onboard amplification options that allow today's musicians to play acoustically or electrically. In addition to guitarmaking, Martin is also one of the world's largest manufacturers of quality musical strings.

family, now and in the future, is fully committed to preserving and extending the vision of C. F. Martin Sr. by continuing to make the finest acoustic guitars in the world.

line of guitars. Today they are the most popular models in the Martin lineup, and virtually every maker of acoustic guitars has attempted to copy the original Martin Dreadnought. While copying cosmetic appearances is relatively easy, copying the tone of a Martin is far more difficult.

LEGACY

Representing the sixth generation of the Martin family to run the business, Chris Martin has led the company through three decades of unprecedented growth and success. About the company's current products, he states, "The guitars we're building today, I believe, are among the best in our company's history — models for every taste and playing style, from the traditional to the most avant-garde. When future generations look back at what we've done, I want them to see how much of our great tradition we have

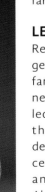

LOOKING AHEAD

Martin's steadfast adherence to high standards of musical excellence, mixed with some sagacious management, has largely accounted for the company's remarkable longevity. Business conditions and musical trends change over the years, but Martin's attitude toward guitar building does not vary.

In the preface to the 1904 catalog, Frank Henry Martin explained, "It takes care and patience in selecting the materials, laying out the proportions and attending to the details that add to the player's comfort. It takes patience in giving the necessary time to finish every part. A good guitar cannot be built for the price of a poor one, but who regrets the extra cost for a good guitar?"

More than a century has passed since Frank Henry Martin of the family's third generation authored this statement, but it still accurately expresses Martin's ongoing commitment to quality. He would be surprised indeed to see today the business that his grandfather started in 1833. What was once a one-man shop is now an energy-filled facility with more than 600 skilled employees. It all started with a love of wood and music. The extended Martin

▶ Classic Facts & Anecdotes

- **The famous full-bodied Martin Dreadnought guitar, first introduced in 1916, was named after a large class of World War I British battleships.**

- A Martin ukulele accompanied the Admiral Byrd Expedition to the North Pole and was subsequently signed by the entire expedition crew, President Calvin Coolidge, Charles Lindbergh, Thomas Edison, and more than a hundred other dignitaries of the day.

- A Martin "Space Guitar," based upon the compact Backpacker travel guitar, was the first guitar to venture into outer space. It was launched in 1994 aboard the Space Shuttle *Columbia* — "To Boldly Go Where No Guitar Has Gone Before!"

- Martin offers one of the most popular factory tours in the United States. More than 40,000 visitors come to Nazareth, Pennsylvania, every year to see guitars being made and to see Martin's impressive museum and instrument collection.

- Martin guitars tend to improve with age, and historically, so does their value. A top-of-the-line Martin D-45 made prior to World War II with an original selling price of about $300 now can bring up to $300,000 on the vintage instrument market.

Mayflower

THE MARKET

More than 15 million American households move each year. In addition to moving individuals and families, van lines move furniture, fixtures, and equipment for businesses. Some van lines, like Mayflower®, also specialize in moving high-value products such as trade show exhibits, medical equipment, and art. Different from traditional freight carriers, these shipments require specialized handling and equipment that van lines are well equipped to provide.

ACHIEVEMENTS

Mayflower Transit is proud to be the most recognized name in moving. It first earned the distinction in a national survey in 1961 and has continued to earn that distinction ever since.

Mayflower is also the first to achieve many important milestones in the moving industry. In 1940 the company was the first van line to receive 48-state operating authority from the Interstate Commerce Commission, which allowed the company to provide service throughout the country. Mayflower also became

the first transportation company to equip long-distance moving vans with air-ride suspension systems, which later became the industry standard. The company also was the first to equip all of its vans with mobile radios and the first van line to be licensed by the FCC for nationwide mobile radio-telephone van communications.

This innovation expedited transmission of information on van location and plans for pickup and delivery — without the van operator having to stop to place phone or telegraph messages.

HISTORY

Conrad M. Gentry and his friend Don F. Kenworthy founded Mayflower Transit Co. in Indianapolis, Indiana, in July 1927 as an alternative to railroads for customers who were interested in moving their belongings across the country on the newly paved roads. In 1928 Burnside Smith added capital and management expertise, reincorporated the business as Aero Mayflower Transit Company, and set the standard for the new enterprise: "To have the best company ... and the best people ... offering the best services."

During the early 1930s Mayflower entered into agreements with a network of local household goods movers who owned storage warehouses and therefore was able to provide

customers with better service at both origin and destination. By 1932, 85 agents adorned their vans with Mayflower's trademarked logo and painted them in Mayflower's vivid colors. As the decade ended, annual revenues neared the $2 million mark, and more than 340 agents became affiliated with Mayflower.

Operating on a 24-hour schedule, Mayflower moved thousands of families of industrial and military personnel who were being mobilized during World War II. When the war ended, America and Mayflower prospered.

In 1952 Mayflower launched another initiative to add to the company's capacity and increase the efficiency of its operation: "owner operators" who owned their own tractors but pulled

Mayflower-owned trailers. Mayflower also established new standards for protecting household goods by eliminating the shredded paper and wooden barrels of the past and introducing new scientifically sized, corrugated cushion packs, along with the Mayflower slogan "Packed with Pride."

As business continued to expand beyond household goods shipping, Mayflower established a special fleet of van operators and vehicles to handle sensitive shipments such as complex computer systems, electronics, and high-tech exhibits.

In 1986 Aero Mayflower became Mayflower Transit Inc. The 1990s brought further significant changes to Mayflower. The van line updated its image through the application of a dramatic new paint scheme for its vans and signage. National studies confirmed that Mayflower had the highest unaided brand name recognition in the moving industry. In March 1995 it was acquired by UniGroup, becoming part of the nation's largest moving and storage services provider.

As Mayflower turned the calendar page into a new century, its fortunes appeared brighter than ever, with the best-known name in the moving industry, improved volume in key business segments, agents embracing the hauling aspect of moving and qualifying for associated revenues, a board of directors composed entirely of agents, and a management team committed to the future of Mayflower as a viable part of the UniGroup family of companies.

THE PRODUCT
From full-service to do-it-yourself moving and storage, Mayflower offers professional moving services. Customers can choose to move with a

portable container and pack and load their goods at their own pace or select a full-service move, with many options in between. Customers can choose from Mayflower's menu of services to fit any relocation need.

In addition to moving household goods, Mayflower also provides transportation for products that require specialized handling, including electronic equipment, trade show exhibits, medical equipment, and works of art.

RECENT DEVELOPMENTS
Mayflower offers portable moving and storage containers under the Mayflower brand. Mayflower containers are now available in most major metropolitan areas across the United States. They offer an effective and economical solution for moving locally or long-distance as well as for storage needs when moving or remodeling. A container is delivered to a customer's home, where customers can pack and load at their own pace. If they need help with the heavy lifting, Mayflower's unique Do-It-Yourself Plus service gives customers the option to get help loading and unloading the items they would prefer not to handle themselves.

PROMOTION
Discover America. Discover America is a community program developed to support schools in the community. It enables fourth- and fifth-grade students to meet a Mayflower van operator and tour his van. Personifying the character of "Driver Bob," the driver promises to correspond with the students as he travels across the country. Each month, students receive thought-provoking letters, postcards, souvenirs, and other information that highlight the geographical features of the country and historically significant events.

Students receive firsthand accounts of Driver Bob's trips and apply the information to the textbook curriculum. Teachers, meanwhile, have an opportunity to develop a fresh approach to daily lessons, based on the Discover America program. Although the program was initially presented to enhance students' awareness and understanding of geography, the program also helps to develop mathematical skills, strengthen creative writing abilities, build career awareness, and teach students about safety precautions.

Internet Marketing. Mayflower employs search engine marketing as an effective way to promote itself to potential customers. By optimizing its presence on the Web, Mayflower allows people to find contact information quickly. Through a unique system, customers are able to easily contact Mayflower's call center and immediately book an appointment with a local Mayflower agent for an in-home estimate.

BRAND VALUES
Mayflower is the trusted brand that Americans have turned to for moving services for more than 80 years. Mayflower introduced updated branding earlier this decade with a new logo and tagline. The logo combines the iconic Mayflower ship with an updated design, color scheme, and font. The branding changes provide a fresh approach while drawing on the heritage of the company's long and rich history.

The tagline, "Mayflower. Every step of the way." conveys the philosophy of Mayflower's careful and trusted movers and the company's dedication to serving its customers throughout every phase of the moving process. The tagline was introduced in a television commercial featuring Mayflower movers moving a 20-foot-tall marionette. The movers carefully guide her through each step as she moves from one home to another.

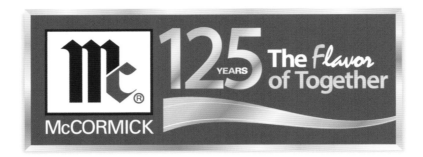

HISTORY

From humble roots in Baltimore, in a single room with just three employees, McCormick's has grown to become a global leader in flavor and the world's largest producer of herbs, spices and seasonings, recipe mixes, and extracts. The company celebrated its 125th anniversary in 2014.

McCormick's history began in 1889 when Willoughby McCormick sold root beer extract door-to-door and penned the memorable slogan, "Make the Best — Someone Will Buy It." Devastation hit when the Great Baltimore Fire of 1904 swept through the city, burning all of the company's material assets and records. Through hard work and sheer determination, Willoughby was able to rebuild the company quickly. Within 10 months, a new five-story building was erected on the old site.

When Willoughby died suddenly in 1932, his 36-year-old nephew, Charles Perry (C. P.) McCormick, was elected president and chairman. C.P. successfully led the company through the Great Depression and to great heights as a global enterprise by the time he retired in 1969.

McCormick stock began trading on the New York Stock Exchange in 1999. Since then, the company's business and product portfolio has changed over time. Growth through geographic expansion and acquisitions is a strategy that remains today. Leading brands in the Americas include McCormick®, Lawry's, Club House, and OLD BAY. New Orleans' favorite Zatarain's, another McCormick brand, also celebrated its 125th anniversary in 2014.

In Europe, the company's major brands include Ducros in France, Schwartz in the United Kingdom, and Kamis® in Poland. Vahiné is a leading dessert aid brand in France. McCormick has been present in China for many years with the McCormick consumer brand. In Central China, Daqiao® and ChuShiLe® are the company's leading brands of bouillon. Down Under, McCormick consumer brands enhance flavor in Australia and New Zealand, while Aeroplane® Jelly is considered Australia's favorite gelatin dessert.

ACHIEVEMENTS

As a global flavor leader, McCormick & Company has — like no other company in the world — a taste for what and how the world eats. McCormick's rich heritage of bringing people together through the universal language of flavor has inspired memorable food experiences while providing the taste behind family traditions passed down from generation to generation.

Still based in Maryland, and with more than $4 billion in annual sales and over 8,000 employees worldwide, McCormick manufactures, markets, and distributes spices, seasoning mixes, condiments, and other flavorful products to the entire food industry — retail outlets, food manufacturers, and foodservice businesses — in more than 140 countries and territories. Innovation in flavor and a clear focus on employee engagement and product quality have allowed McCormick to grow its business globally and become the flavor leader it is today.

More than 125 years later, McCormick continues to bring passion to its work, and the entire company pulls together to make the difference — with a passion for flavor, a uniquely collaborative culture, and high-quality flavors and spices. McCormick founder Willoughby McCormick's motto, "Make the Best — Someone Will Buy It," is still a critical value for the company.

At the foundation of McCormick's values are the company's five pillars of success:

- Passion for flavor®
- Power of people®
- Taste you trust®
- Inspiring healthy choices
- Delivering high performance

LEGACY

McCormick's longevity can be attributed not only to financial performance but also its unique collaborative culture, introduced long before it was the norm and maintained through difficult

economic times. C. P. McCormick, a pioneer in participative management, understood the powerful results that a company can achieve when employees collaborate and work beyond their line function to help solve big issues. Building on this knowledge, as CEO he established the Multiple Management Board in 1932. The program and culture are so successful, McCormick's Global Multiple Management Board was recognized by Human Resource Executive Online as one of the Best HR Ideas for 2012 — an eight-decade-old "idea" still working today. As an active civic leader, C.P.'s impact was felt locally,

nationally, and globally. His belief in giving back remains a core company value.

McCormick's unique and collaborative culture is also recognized through the numerous supplier and partner awards the teams win globally from their industrial and retail customers.

Many of McCormick's top brands are not only regional leaders — brands with a leading share in a market — but they also share a strong heritage: Club House®, 134 years; Zatarain's®, 128 years; Billy Bee®, 59 years; Ducros®, 54 years; Vahiné®,

45 years; Aeroplane®, 100 years; Lawry's®, 79 years; Schwartz®, 176 years; and OLD BAY®, 78 years.

And McCormick's has an influence on consumers' palates far beyond its own brands. McCormick's creates custom flavor solutions for nine of the top 10 food and beverage companies and each of the top 10 foodservice restaurant chains in the United States.

LOOKING AHEAD

One of McCormick's most groundbreaking innovations to date is FlavorPrint™. This breakthrough interactive service provides personalized recipe and product recommendations for the foods consumers already love — and the new favorites they are about to discover. The more consumers engage, the smarter the service becomes, resulting in personalized recommendations and an enhanced ongoing experience. This one-on-one conversation with consumers allows McCormick to develop relationships in ways that would never before have been possible. From suggesting better recipes during health and wellness season and identifying personalized grilling recipes to helping plan holiday dinners, FlavorPrint™ offers an added layer of custom engagement that consumers are craving.

FlavorPrint™ has already garnered a number of prestigious awards, including a pair of Global Cannes Lion awards: a Silver Cyber Lion for branded utility/tool and a Bronze Cyber Lion for user experience. McCormick also received a Bronze London International Award for the digital/foods category and a Silver IAB International Mix award for branded utility.

Since 2000, McCormick experts have also been predicting flavor trends through its Flavor

Forecast®. The McCormick® Flavor Forecast® highlights top food insights and emerging flavors predicted to impact the way the world will eat in the coming years — a challenge with today's unparalleled connectivity, which drives faster-than-ever adoption of new trends and tastes around the globe. For 2016, for example, the trends included

- Heat + Tang
- Tropical Asian
- Alternative "Pulse" Proteins
- Blends with Benefits
- Ancestral Flavors
- Culinary-Infused Sips

Classic Facts and Anecdotes

- McCormick and Zatarain's not only began the same year — 1889 — the two companies also sold the same product: root beer extract. Zatarain's joined the McCormick family of brands in 2003.

- Two-thirds of McCormick's consumer business sales are from brands that are number one in their category.

- McCormick products can make up 90 percent of a meal's flavor and just 10 percent of the cost.

- Aeroplane Jelly from Australia entered the Guinness World Records in 1981 by making the largest-ever gelatin. It was watermelon flavored and 35,000 liters (9,246.02 gallons).

- McCormick Brand is America's favorite vanilla extract.

HISTORY

Baseball's first professional team was founded in Cincinnati in 1869, 30 years after Abner Doubleday supposedly invented the game of baseball. The first few decades of professional baseball were characterized by rivalries between leagues and by players who often jumped from one team or league to another. The period before 1920 in baseball was known as the dead-ball era; players rarely hit home runs during this time. Baseball survived a conspiracy to fix the 1919 World Series, which came to be known as the Black Sox Scandal. The sport rose in popularity in the 1920s and survived potential downturns during the Great Depression and World War II. Shortly after the war, Jackie Robinson broke baseball's color barrier.

The 1950s and 1960s were a time of expansion for the AL and NL, then new stadiums and artificial turf surfaces began to change the game in the 1970s and 1980s. Home runs dominated the game during the 1990s, and media reports began to discuss the use of anabolic steroids among Major League players in the mid-2000s. In 2006, an investigation produced the Mitchell Report, which implicated many players in the use of performance-enhancing substances, including at least one player from each team.

Today, MLB is composed of 30 teams: 29 in the United States and one in Canada. Teams play

162 games each season, and five teams in each league advance to a four-round postseason tournament that culminates in the World Series, a best-of-seven championship series between the two league champions that dates to 1903. Baseball broadcasts are aired on television, radio, and the Internet throughout North America and in several other countries throughout the world. MLB has the highest season attendance of any sports league in the world, with more than 73 million spectators in 2016.

ACHIEVEMENTS

More than 60 percent of Americans consider themselves fans of Major League Baseball, which is a true source of family-friendly entertainment. Due to that national appeal, some of the most recognizable brands in the world — including Nike, Bank of America, Pepsi, Anheuser-Busch, MasterCard, Chevrolet, T-Mobile, and Gatorade — are MLB partners.

Major League Baseball's international presence continues to grow. MLB games are broadcast in Spanish throughout Latin America. Games also air in

Australia, and have appeared in the United Kingdom as well. The Arizona Diamondbacks opened the 2014 season against Los Angeles Dodgers March 22–23 in Australia. The teams played each other at the historic Sydney Cricket Ground, which has a seating capacity of 46,000.

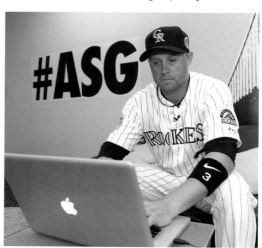

The two games represented the first MLB regular-season play held in that country, and the games counted as home games for the Diamondbacks.

Together with the World Baseball Softball Confederation, MLB sponsors the international World Baseball Classic. The tournament is the

first of its kind to have the national teams of the International Baseball Federation's member federations feature professional players from leagues around the world, including Major League Baseball. In addition to providing a format for the world's best baseball players to compete against one another while representing their home countries, the World Baseball Classic was created in order to further promote the game around the globe. After a three-year gap between the first two installments of the tournament, plans were made for the World Baseball Classic to be repeated every four years following the 2009 event. The third installment of the Classic was held in 2013, and the fourth took place in March 2017.

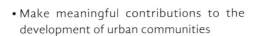

LEGACY

MLB is a social institution, with important responsibilities to fans and communities. Led by the vision of Commissioner Allan H. (Bud) Selig, MLB has taken extraordinary steps to give back to communities. This commitment is evidenced by baseball's dedication to advancing important causes, including youth access to sport, support for veterans in their return to civilian life, and the fight against cancer. MLB champions these important causes through programs and partnerships with a wide variety of organizations, including Autism Awareness, Boys and Girls Clubs of America, 4ALS, and Welcome Back Veterans.

Urban Youth Academy. Major League Baseball's first Urban Youth Academy was founded in 2006 in Compton, California. As a not-for-profit organization, the UYA aims to set the standard for baseball and softball instruction, teach and educate in urban America, and enhance the quality of life in its surrounding communities. Major League Baseball has set out four components for the Urban Youth Academy:

- Grow the games of baseball and softball while cultivating diversity in all aspects of the game

- Make meaningful contributions to the development of urban communities
- Provide safe and organized recreational activities for urban youth
- Prepare urban high school players for college and professional baseball and softball programs

Baseball Tomorrow Fund. The Baseball Tomorrow Fund (BTF) is a joint initiative between Major League Baseball and the Major League Baseball Players Association (MLBPA). The fund awards grants to organizations involved in the operation of youth baseball and softball programs and facilities. BTF's mission is to promote and enhance the growth of youth participation in baseball and softball throughout the world. BTF funds programs, fields, coaches' training and uniforms, equipment, and other selected program expenses. In addition, BTF provides educational support to grant recipients and applicants, to help organizations become self-sufficient and effective.

Announced during the 1999 World Series, the Baseball Tomorrow Fund began with a $10 million commitment by MLB and the MLBPA. Since then, both parties have agreed to additional, annual contributions that have more than tripled the original commitment. BTF awards grants on a quarterly basis. The fund awards an average of 55 grants per year, averaging more than $1.8 million annually. BTF has awarded over 900 grants totaling more than $30 million to nonprofit and tax-exempt organizations

in the United States, Canada, Latin America, the Caribbean, Europe, and Asia.

LOOKING AHEAD

Baseball has been celebrated as the national pastime for more than a century, holding a unique place in the cultural fabric of American society and in the lives of fans. Major League Baseball is the protector and promoter of this great game, ensuring that the sport continues to develop, prosper, and evoke powerful memories and emotions for years to come.

▶ Classic Facts and Anecdotes

- The Atlanta Braves — previously of Milwaukee and Boston — are the only franchise to have played continuously since the inauguration of the National Association in 1871.

- As of publication time, 72 players in Major League Baseball history have had six hits in one game (of those, 9 were seven-hit games).

- Baltimore Orioles shortstop Cal Ripken Jr. didn't miss a game in 16 years. He played in 2,632 consecutive games from April 30, 1982, to September 19, 1998.

- During World War II, the US military designed a grenade to be the size and weight of a baseball, since "any young American man should be able to properly throw it."

- Every MLB baseball is rubbed in Lena Blackburne Baseball Rubbing Mud, a unique "very fine" mud only found in a secret location near Palmyra, New Jersey.

- The world's largest publicly available collection of baseball cards is housed at the Metropolitan Museum of Art. It has over 31,000 cards.

HISTORY

Plenty of great ideas have come out of bars. Though when saloon-keeper James Ritty invented the world's first cash register, he probably had no idea where his idea would lead. From a device for automatically recording sales to technological achievements that smooth the movements of worldwide commerce, NCR's story of growth, achievement, and influence has few parallels.

Enamored with Ritty's invention, John H. Patterson bought two cash registers for his miners' supply store. In six months, the registers helped reduce his debt and generate a profit. Further convinced of the machine's potential, Patterson bought the National Manufacturing Company, producer of the cash registers, in 1884 and renamed it the National Cash Register Company. Today that company is the NCR Corporation.

NCR almost has too many firsts to mention — many of them far afield from the humble beginnings of a cash register. Pioneering modern salesmanship and direct marketing, producing the world's first sales manual and the first newspaper for employees, promoting women in management, implementing the world's first employee suggestion system, and taking bold and novel steps to improve workers' conditions . . . credit them all to NCR.

Technologically, it's difficult to overestimate NCR's influence on daily life. In 1954 NCR scientist Barrett Green invented the micro-encapsulation process, making time-release

medications possible. John Janning invented the thermal printing wafer, kicking off the process that led to digital fax technology. Janning also perfected liquid crystal displays (LCDs) in 1968, which helped give birth to calculators, digital watches, and hand-held video games. Today the company's main products include point-of-sale terminals, automated teller machines, and scanners. NCR is also active in financial services, retail, hospitality, travel, telecom, small businesses, and the public sector. In fact, NCR is the world leader in consumer transaction technologies.

Incorporated in 1900, NCR was acquired by AT&T in 1991, but the company was reestablished on January 1, 1997, as a separate entity. NCR is the only AT&T spinoff that has retained its original name; all the others have either been purchased or renamed following subsequent mergers. The company has also retained its iconic logo, developed in 1996 by renowned graphic designer Saul Bass.

The company's headquarters are in metropolitan Atlanta, having moved from its historical home in Dayton, Ohio. Serving as NCR's CEO since 2005, Bill Nuti states, "We are running commerce around the globe in a way that no other company frankly can proclaim."

ACHIEVEMENTS

NCR's position as a technology leader is unquestioned. The company holds 2,600 patents (1,400 in the United States) and has more than 1,700 pending patent applications. Among the company's accomplishments are as follows:

NCR was the first company to market a product to prevent fraud. The cash register, or "incorruptible cashier," helped retailers keep a record of incoming cash — and prevented employees from pocketing it.

Three days after John H. Patterson purchased the virtually bankrupt National Manufacturing Company, he began to contact sales agents around the country because he had no money for salaries. Agents didn't want to sell on a full-time basis until he gave each of them an exclusive territory — at the time an unknown approach to marketing.

Patterson also made NCR the original home of direct marketing. He believed that "sales make news. And news of sales makes more sales." To develop a direct mailing list, Patterson asked NCR agents to collect business cards from their prospects. A typist pool addressed labels for direct mail advertising.

NCR's first significant diversification effort began in the 1920s with the Class 2000 accounting machine, a sophisticated cash register that printed data on inserted forms and provided 30 totals. Product evolution moved toward more complex transaction processing for users in retail, hotels, railroads, banking, and other industries — a partial forecast of where the company would be a century later.

Each year, businesses and consumers recognize NCR for excellence. Some examples are as follows:

NCR is committed to conducting all aspects of business in an environmentally sound manner worldwide, striving to minimize the environmental footprint of its operations and products, while delivering innovative technologies and solutions designed to help businesses and consumers reduce their own environmental footprint.

- NCR's two-sided thermal receipt printing technology (2ST) allows simultaneous printing on both sides of a thermal paper receipt or document, to reduce paper usage by almost half.

- The European Union Directive on the Restriction of the use of certain Hazardous Substances (RoHS) limits the use of lead, mercury, cadmium, hexavalent chromium, polybrominated biphenyls (PBB), and polybrominated diphenyl ethers (PBDE) in electrical and electronic equipment placed on the European Community market. NCR is fully compliant with the EU RoHS Directive and similar legislation in other regions, such as China and the state of California.

- NCR's end-of-life hardware management services ensure secure and environmentally responsible product decommissioning, recycling, treatment, and compliant disposal. The company's decommissioning and recycling programs are compliant with international recycling legislation.

- NCR's Columbus, Georgia, facility was one of the very first LEED-certified retrofitted manufacturing plants in the United States.

Reputation Institute named NCR among America's most reputable companies in the technology industry in July 2015. NCR ranked number 7 overall on the 2015 list of America's top 25 most reputable technology companies, ahead of some of the most recognizable brands in the world.

Forbes magazine named NCR as one of America's best employers for 2015 in the magazine's first-ever Top Employer list.

NCR and First National Bank won the award for "Best ATM and Kiosk Project in Africa" at the *Asian Banker*'s Middle East and Africa Country 2014 Award ceremony.

NCR is the world leader in self-checkout (SCO) technology, according to strategic research and consulting firm RBR. NCR was the 2013 leader in SCO shipments with a 71 percent share, more than double the number of SCO shipments for all other competitors combined.

NCR announced a formal partnership with the NFL's Atlanta Falcons in 2013, providing POS software for Falcons' merchandise, including mobile point of sale to the Falcons and creating innovative experiences such as in-suite ordering and postgame merchandise pickup. Wayfinding touchscreen technology from NCR also helps fans navigate Falcons' game days. The two organizations partnered on a variety of community initiatives, including an internship program. NCR announced in October 2015 that it would also be one of the 14 founding partners of Atlanta's new Mercedes-Benz Stadium.

LEGACY

NCR's effect on global business is obvious in a numerical sense, but American workers can trace many improvements in working conditions back to John Patterson.

Early in Patterson's industrial career a shipment of cash registers was returned to the factory from England because of defective workmanship. With such a blow to the company's prestige and profit, Patterson acted typically for him, moving his desk into the factory to discover what was wrong. He found more than he expected, and the results were likely more long-lasting than intended.

When he first acquired NCR, Patterson found that the factory conditions needed to be drastically improved. The factory was cleaned. Each worker had his individual locker. The men were satisfied. No more defective cash registers came back.

Patterson learned then that close contact with his factory force was the basis of real industrial relations. That first dingy workroom led Patterson to introduce the first American daylight factory, with 80 percent of the walls consisting of glass windows. His formula for working conditions and labor relations henceforth embodied the three elements of head, hand, and heart. They were the expression of practical altruism and spelled business success.

Back in the 19th century, few business leaders gave much thought to improving employees' lives. But one day, not long after the episode with the returned cash registers, Patterson saw a woman factory worker warming a pot of coffee on a radiator. It gave him the inspiration to provide hot meals for employees.

Thus began the era of employee benefits in American industry. The hot meals were followed by rest periods, dining rooms, medical service with a dental clinic, visiting nurses, health education, recreational grounds, motion pictures during lunch, clubs for employees, night classes, vacations, and educational trips.

Well-educated working women could also expect to advance quickly to supervisory roles within NCR. Amy Acton, who became NCR's counselor-at-law in 1890, is believed to be the first woman lawyer hired by a corporation — at a time long before women in the United States were even allowed to vote.

NCR employees give back as well. To celebrate the 130th anniversary of NCR's founding, NCR Ambassadors, a group of 300 employees in nearly 100 locations who share a passion for NCR and making a difference in their communities, encouraged NCR employees to complete volunteer service during a 130-hour period starting on Monday, November 3, 2014, and ending on Saturday, November 8. The Ambassadors organized the "Big Give" in 2013, in which NCR employees donated nearly 20,000 hours of their time to worthy causes.

LOOKING AHEAD

NCR has always been ahead of its time, and changes come so fast these days that only the hardiest of companies can remain on the necessary cutting edge. NCR is moving its business from hardware-driven solutions to cloud-mobile, software-based solutions — still backed by the best available hardware.

Such repositioning also means a greatly expanded available market opportunity for NCR,

to an estimated $87 billion (as of 2015). As the global leader in consumer transaction technologies, NCR turns everyday interactions with businesses into exceptional experiences, making life easier along the way.

▶ Classic Facts and Anecdotes

- Starting in 1887, NCR sales agents were required to memorize a 450-word primer based on the successful sales presentation of Joseph H. Crane, John H. Patterson's brother-in-law, whose sales record consistently topped the other agents.

- NCR engineers invented scratch-and-sniff technology.

- NCR is the only company that sells its own receipt rolls to go with point-of-service and automated teller machines.

- Charles F. Kettering, an NCR employee, developed the first electric cash register. Kettering later worked for General Motors and invented the electric car starter.

- In 1974 NCR commercialized bar code scanners. For the world's first Universal Product Code (UPC) scanner, installed at Marsh's Supermarket in Troy, Ohio, the first scanned item was a package of Wrigley's Juicy Fruit chewing gum.

- NCR helps over 550 million transactions take place every day.

HISTORY

The world-famous OREO cookie brand has been delighting consumers for more than 100 years. In the early 1910s, English-style biscuits were popular among American consumers. The National Biscuit Company produced the first OREO cookie in late February 1912, and the first sale took place on March 6 to a Hoboken shopkeeper named S. C. Thuesen.

Distributed in bulk tins with glass tops, consumers could actually see the cookies inside. The ensuing century would prove OREO cookies were ready for the big stage, as they soon grew from a local favorite to a global cookie icon.

Speculation, though, still surrounds the meaning of the OREO name. One school of thought holds that the inspiration came from the Greek word *oreo,* meaning "hill" or "mountain," reflecting the mounded shape of some early test versions. Since the original label had considerable gold scroll work on the pale green background, others believe that the name comes from the French word *or,* which means "gold." Others say that OREO is a combination of "re" from the word "cream," surrounded by the double "O" shapes of the cookies. Some people take a more direct approach: Nabisco founder Adolphus Green simply liked the sound of the name "OREO."

ACHIEVEMENTS

OREO, "Milk's Favorite Cookie," has proven to be an industry leader not just in the United States but around the world. Currently about a $1 billion brand, OREO continues to thrive, outpacing the competition domestically and internationally. As a beloved brand with successful new product launches, OREO has become a cornerstone for parent company Mondelez International. OREO cookies are available on shelves in more than 100 countries.

Throughout the years, the brand has brought to life the powerful OREO and milk connection in a number of innovative advertising and promotional channels. One unique example is a panoramic elevator in a shopping mall that dramatizes the traditional OREO and milk connection: a picture of an OREO cookie on the elevator dunks into a glass of milk as the elevator descends. Because the OREO and milk moment is central to the brand's identity, the advertising tagline was switched from "America's Favorite Cookie" to "Milk's Favorite Cookie."

Another unique trait of OREO is the brand's unified worldwide marketing strategy. While the communications are translated and adapted for local cultures, the core communication of special moments of childlike delight enabled by the TWIST, LICK, AND DUNK ritual using an OREO and milk is consistent across the globe.

With significant investment in promotions and public relations, the OREO brand has forged strong, lasting connections with consumers. Two signature marketing programs have been the OREO Global Moments contest and the Double Stuf Racing League.

In 2008 the brand hosted the OREO Global Moments contest, which asked OREO fans around the world to submit videos depicting a special OREO and Milk Moment. Consumers from eight different countries on four different continents entered videos depicting a wide range of OREO and Milk Moments. From original OREO-themed songs and animated skits to family lessons on OREO dunking techniques, fans showed their passion for the brand with every video submission. The winning video, which depicted a little girl giving her last OREO cookie

and a glass of milk to a soldier, was featured on the YouTube homepage for a day.

OREO energized the popular act of twisting, licking, and dunking by launching the Double Stuf Racing League ("DSRL"). The DSRL represented a different way to enjoy the classic OREO cookie and milk ritual. It's a fun activity that family and friends can still enjoy together, racing to see who can finish an OREO DOUBLE STUF cookie and glass of milk the fastest. Racers twist their cookie open, lick off all the creme, dunk it in milk, eat the cookie, and drink the glass of milk. The first to finish twisting, licking, and dunking wins. Commercials featured numerous celebrity athletes as DSRL athletes, driving significant media attention to the unique campaign and resulting in positive, long-lasting consumer response. OREO DOUBLE STUF consumption grew significantly after the launch of the DSRL in 2008.

In keeping with the changing media landscape, OREO has elevated its strategy by connecting millions of passionate fans to each other (and the brand) through social media networks such as Facebook, Twitter, and YouTube — ideal tools for a brand like OREO, whose strategy is rooted in connecting family and friends. The brand's foundation of connections in combination with the global reach of OREO lend credibility to the two-way conversations that social media platforms enable on a daily basis.

Consumers who "like" OREO on Facebook also receive brand updates, such as exclusive behind-the-scenes content from OREO advertising shoots and new product news. By embracing the new opportunity to connect with consumers, OREO has emerged as a leader in social media and, in late 2016, was the sixth-most-liked brand on Facebook. For perspective, three of the

top five were Facebook itself, YouTube, and Microsoft Windows.

Whether it's through social media or lick racing contests, OREO is reaching consumers through award-winning advertisements, unique promotions, and public relation campaigns that continue to build the OREO brand equity.

LEGACY

Since the turn of the millennium, the OREO brand continues to deliver on its strong equities,

while also expanding to fill new consumer demands. In the mid-1970s OREO DOUBLE STUF cookies were introduced at the request of consumers who sought more creme filling. In 1987 OREO entered the indulgent segment of the market with a fudge-covered version. In response to consumers' desire for bite-sized, snackable foods they could eat on the go, OREO developed Mini OREO sandwich cookies in 1991. Following health and wellness consumer trends, OREO introduced Sugar-Free and Reduced Fat varieties. Additional varieties now include Peanut Butter, Chocolate, and Cool Mint creme flavors. Every year, consumers eagerly await special seasonal varieties of OREO for winter, spring, and Halloween. Limited-edition flavors also appear regularly and have included Key Lime Pie, Pumpkin Spice Oreo, and Fruity Crisp, made of two golden OREO cookies with a colorful rice crisp cream filling.

In recent years, the OREO brand has emphasized promotion to emerge as a national and global powerhouse. The OREO brand extended its equity into a variety of different product forms, including chocolate-covered varieties and "Golden" vanilla-flavored wafers. Licensing also became a key brand builder for OREO. Licensed products — including cheesecake, ice cream, and baking products — allowed consumers to connect with the OREO brand in a novel fashion.

The OREO brand represents more than a cookie. It delivers more than a delicious snack. The form of an OREO cookie — two delicious wafers brought together and joined by sweet creme filling — provides a unique metaphor for the memorable moments of connection that the iconic cookie can produce among family and friends, spanning generations and borders. From a grandfather sharing milk and OREO cookies with his beloved granddaughter to a boy teaching his younger brother how to twist, lick, and dunk an OREO, a connection happens whenever you share a moment over OREO cookies.

LOOKING AHEAD

After a century on the shelves, OREO has a special place in the hearts and homes of cookie fans of all ages. While "Milk's Favorite Cookie" is as good as it was in 1912, the OREO brand continues to evolve and grow — adding new markets, new products, and new channels for its loyal fans around the globe.

Key factors in the continued growth of OREO are the brand's award-winning advertising and best-in-class consumer promotions. The brand's approach to engaging consumers stays true to its essence: creating

connections through the classic OREO and milk ritual that brings people together in moments of childlike delight. Whether it's twisting, licking, dunking, or a combination of all three, OREO offers everyday moments of connection that other snack brands cannot match.

▶ Classic Facts and Anecdotes

- OREO cookies cost just 30 cents a pound when they were introduced.

- Among the nations where consumers can buy an OREO are Australia, China, Chile, Indonesia, Morocco, Poland, and Germany.

- Since its introduction in 2003, GOLDEN OREO has grown to become the number-one brand in the golden sandwich cookie category.

- The National Biscuit Company factory where OREO cookies were first developed and produced was on Ninth Avenue between 15th and 16th Streets in New York City. Today, this same block of Ninth Avenue is known as "Oreo Way."

THE PHILADELPHIA CONTRIBUTIONSHIP

HISTORY

In 1752, before the United States was fully established, Philadelphia was a bustling Delaware River port city of over 15,000 residents. The risk of fire was constant, and the city was ill-prepared to handle it. When a 1730 fire destroyed all of the stores and a number of homes on Fishbourn's wharf, the city purchased firefighting equipment and distributed it around the city. However, Benjamin Franklin, who was Philadelphia's foremost proponent of fire prevention, recognized that having the equipment was not enough and that the city's greatest weakness in fire defense was the disorganized firefighting efforts of its citizens. To remedy that situation, in 1736 Franklin formed what would become the first volunteer fire company in America, the Union Fire Company.

At a meeting of the Union Fire Company in 1751, the idea of an insurance plan was first introduced. Franklin and a silversmith, Phillip Syng — the same man who fashioned the inkstand used in the signing of the Declaration of Independence — met with representatives of six other firefighting companies to discuss the insurance idea. The group agreed to move the idea forward.

By February 1752 a notice appeared in Franklin's newspaper, the *Pennsylvania Gazette*, announcing that a new business venture was forming and all Philadelphians were invited to the courthouse to learn more. The announcement read, "All persons inclined to subscribe to the articles of insurance of houses from fire, in or near this city, are desired to appear at the Court House, where attendance will be given, to take in their subscriptions, every seventh day of the week, in the afternoon, until the 13th of April next, being the day appointed by the said articles for electing twelve directors and a treasurer." On April 13, there was enough interest to call a

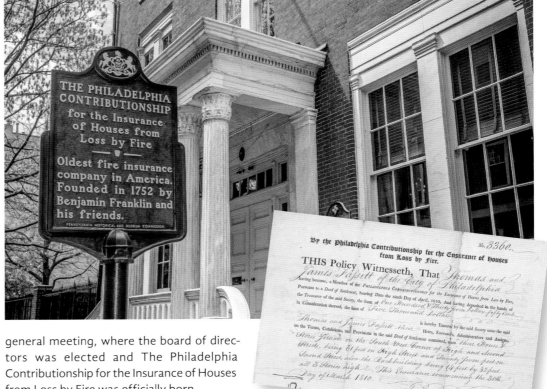

general meeting, where the board of directors was elected and The Philadelphia Contributionship for the Insurance of Houses from Loss by Fire was officially born.

The first policy, protecting a home against fire loss, was issued in June 1752, and the first loss did not occur until more than a year later. Each new insurer added a signature to the Deed of Settlement, a document engrossed on 15 feet of parchment. The company's policyholders were prominent citizens of the time, including three signers of the Declaration of Independence — John Morton, Robert Morris, and Ben Franklin — as well as the fourth president of the United States, James Madison.

ACHIEVEMENTS

The Philadelphia Contributionship continued to grow as the nation

developed. At the end of the first 100 years of operation, the company had accumulated $694,000 in assets, with insured values totaling just under $8 million. But there was considerable unrest and uncertainty as the Civil War approached. The war significantly affected Philadelphia and the Contributionship, as the city served as an entry point to the South. The company provided financial and moral support to the troops by purchasing war bonds and making contributions to various causes — such as the Citizens Bounty Fund, which

encouraged enlistments — providing refreshments to soldiers, and assisting individual military units. In 1863, when the city was threatened during the Battle of Gettysburg, the Contributionship held a special meeting and agreed to donate $20,000 toward the defense of the city.

Eight decades later, the company was again deeply affected by war: World War II. The staff was nearly depleted when employees joined the war effort. Two men joined the army, two men joined the navy, one woman joined the Women's Army Corps, and one woman, Harriet Matlack, joined the navy's Women Accepted for Voluntary Emergency Service (WAVES). She ultimately served as the secretary to Admiral Chester W. Nimitz, who was commander-in-chief of the US Navy's Pacific Fleet. Despite a lean staff, the Contributionship endured the war years intact, and by the end of 1945, the company had assets of $13 million and a surplus of nearly $11 million.

In 1976 the nation and Philadelphia celebrated the bicentennial of the Declaration of Independence. The Contributionship's major donations went toward development of the

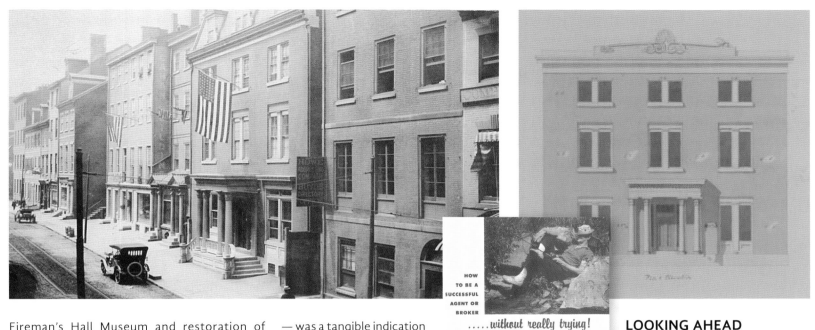

Fireman's Hall Museum and restoration of Pennsylvania Hospital. The company's own building, certified as a historical landmark by the city of Philadelphia in 1956, received the highest honor in 1979 when the National Park Service designated it a National Historic Landmark.

The Bicentennial of the Constitution in 1987 gave rise to more celebrations, and the company took part in the commissioning ceremonies for the USS *Thomas S. Gates,* a new naval warship named in honor of one of the Contributionship's former directors.

As the company moved through the 1980s, business operations were expanded into New Jersey. The company also acquired various security companies, which combined to become Vector Security, the ninth-largest home and commercial security monitoring company in the country.

At the close of 2015 The Philadelphia Contributionship remains a mutual company that is now represented in Pennsylvania, New Jersey, Delaware, and Maryland. The company continues to exclusively insure homes, property, and associated liability. The Contributionship holds current assets of $440 million and surplus of $245 million, and it remains the oldest successful property and casualty company in the country.

LEGACY
The Philadelphia Contributionship's greatest legacy is the creation of the mutual insurance industry in America — and with it, the concept of continuing coverage. The company served as a model for many of the mutual companies that followed. Over the centuries, the Contributionship supported the free exchange of information among those in the industry, through correspondence and later education through the establishment of insurance-related organizations.

To further promote awareness and recognition of the company, the early directors of The Philadelphia Contributionship commissioned the making of America's first fire marks, a plaque or badge placed on the exterior of a building, indicating that it was insured. The introduction of the company fire mark, cast by John Stow — the same man who helped to recast the Liberty Bell

— was a tangible indication of an insured's coverage. The Contributionship's fire mark consists of four-clasped hands because "contribution" was defined in Thomas Sheridan's 1796 dictionary as "that which is given by several hands for some common purpose." The fire mark, which mirrors the company seal, was a visible sign of mutual support where members worked hand in hand to insure each other from loss. This practice, too, was picked up by many of the insurance companies that followed.

The Philadelphia Contributionship's fire mark, as well as many competitors' fire marks, can still be seen on homes in and around the Philadelphia region. The company's name and logo both testify to the fact that, regardless of The Philadelphia Contributionship's growth, the company's mission remains the same: providing insurance protection with exceptional service for its community.

LOOKING AHEAD
The Philadelphia Contributionship's stability and superior service continue to be at the forefront of business practices. As the company looks to the decades ahead, the mission remains providing comprehensive insurance protection and outstanding customer service for the urban and suburban neighbors within the community.

Losses and the future are always unpredictable. Still, the company remains strong as it heads into its next century. There is little in the way of disasters or human nature that it has not survived. Through it all, the Contributionship has remained committed to its policyholders and the community it serves. The Philadelphia Contributionship has not sought to be the largest insurance company in America, but rather to be the best that it can be in rendering its services to those who have placed their faith and trust in the company. The company remains deeply rooted in its history and continuously focused on the future.

◤ Classic Facts and Anecdotes

The Philadelphia Contributionship continued operations during the Revolutionary War — and there was a wide range of opinions within the company on the war. Some were strong Loyalists who saw great value in remaining part of the British Empire, others were prominent leaders in the Patriot cause, and still others were committed to neutrality, as the company's founders were mostly Quakers. The company came through the war years intact, but the division of opinion within the company eventually caused some dissension.

Among the company's early underwriting guidelines was the refusal to insure houses with trees in front because they could hinder firefighting efforts. In 1784, when that requirement was affirmed, some policyholders, rather than cutting down their trees, broke away from the Contributionship and formed the company's first competitor, the Mutual Assurance Company — a company willing to insure homes with trees in front. Because of its stance on trees, the Mutual Assurance Company quickly became known as the Green Tree.

While trees were the given reason for the split, other considerations came into play. Those who formed the Green Tree were deeply involved on the American side of the war, and they saw the need for new businesses in the city to build its economy. Contributing to the growth of the new nation was at least some motivation for the new entity. The Green Tree remained in business until its acquisition in the 1990s.

HISTORY

In 1887, brothers Alfred and George Rawlings founded a sporting goods store in downtown St. Louis, selling everything from wagon covers to parlor games. Over the course of the next 130 years, Rawlings has morphed into a global sporting goods manufacturer committed to product innovation, quality, and authenticity. Rawlings continues to be one of the most prominent brands in its competitive space, appealing to athletes of all ages and abilities.

Long before the famous Rawlings trademark, "The Finest in the Field®," appeared in advertisements featuring Hall of Famers Roberto Clemente, Stan Musial, Mickey Mantle, and Brooks Robinson, it became the foundation for every product line of the company — most notably Rawlings' legendary baseball gloves. Rawlings has continuously redesigned defense with its long history of technological innovations: from the Bill Doak glove introduced in 1919, featuring a built-in pocket and formed web; to the six-fingered Trap-Eze® launched in 1960, the most radical design change in 40 years; to the 2016 ColorSync™ series, which allows players to customize the colors of the iconic Rawlings patch.

But Rawlings' most famous glove has never been for sale. The Rawlings Gold Glove Award® was created in 1957 after Rawlings executive Elmer Blasco noticed during a visit to spring training sites that 83 percent of regular players used Rawlings gloves. Since "The Finest in the Field" was the centerpiece of the company's national advertising campaign, Blasco devised the idea to honor the best defensive players at each position and in each league with the Rawlings Gold Glove Award; at this point in time, baseball's postseason awards focused almost entirely on offensive excellence.

The Rawlings Gold Glove award, similar to Major League Baseball, has evolved immensely over the years. The initial award was constructed from gold tanned leather — ironically, the same leather used to create ladies' formal slippers — from Brown Shoe Company in St. Louis. While the materials may have been unconventional, it came to be one of the most iconic and recognizable awards of the century. In 2007, the 50th anniversary of the award, Rawlings introduced a more modern look to resemble that of a luxury car. The current award features a buried cherry wood base with a lacquered black piano wood trim. Additionally, a section of the award base is covered with Rawlings Heart of the Hide leather embroidered with the Rawlings Patch logo. If Rawlings Gold Glove winners, selected by managers and coaches, are also Rawlings endorsers, they receive a gold version of their game-day model glove on their award.

ACHIEVEMENTS

Some of baseball's most memorable and widely recognized individual achievements featured Rawlings' products:

- Willie Mays's amazing over-the-back catch in Game 1 of the 1954 World Series dropped inside Rawlings leather.

- Mickey Mantle's running catch to save Don Larsen's perfect game in the 1956 World Series landed in his Rawlings Heart of the Hide glove.

- Hank Aaron's record-setting 715th home run launched from a Rawlings Adirondack bat.

- Reggie Jackson's three-home-run performance with a Rawlings bat clinched Game 6 of the 1977 World Series.

- Every one of Mark McGwire's 70 home runs in 1998 came off a Rawlings bat.

RAWLINGS "BILL DOAK" GLOVE
The One Glove With Which Great Players Make Records.

RAWLINGS "BILL DOAK" GLOVE

These and many other Big Leaguers use and prefer to all others
THE RAWLINGS "BILL DOAK" GLOVES

Widely recognized as the "#1 Baseball Brand Worldwide," Rawlings is the exclusive supplier of baseballs to and the official helmet of Major League Baseball, and the top ball-glove choice of more professional players than any other brand in the marketplace today.

In recent history, Rawlings has taken paramount strides to become an elite name in nonwood baseball bats. Through unmatched technological advances and cosmetic perfection, Rawlings has proven to be an industry-leading company in terms of overall consumer satisfaction. Jump-started by the success of the University of South Carolina and the University of Virginia baseball teams, winners of the NCAA® College World Series in 2010 and 2011 (South Carolina) and in 2015 (UVA), respectively, Rawlings' nonwood bat category has continued to solidify as product performance improved.

Rawlings wood bats regained market share at the Major League level in 2015 after investments at the company's Adirondack facility, which produces premier wood bats for the likes of Matt Kemp, Manny Machado, and more than 250 other top Major League and Minor League baseball players. Key additions to the wood bat factory include a new-to-the-industry acoustic grading process, as well as vacuum kiln, core saw, and wood saver technology.

Rawlings recently expanded its Fan Gear category as well, by working in conjunction with sister company Coleman® to produce chairs, coolers, canopies, basketballs, footballs, and novelty baseballs for the NBA, NFL, MLB, and NCAA.

As baseball's social marketing leader, Rawlings continues to engage consumers, retailers, and strategic partners in innovative ways through daily engagements, exclusive experiences, and exemplary customer service. These digital grassroots initiatives convert passive observers and "likes" into active community participants and brand advocates to help Rawlings engage and enable consumers directly.

LEGACY
Due to its market share and player-preferred position in the marketplace, Rawlings is "The Mark of a Pro®," and the famous Rawlings Red Label Design® and Rawlings Script are synonymous with the best of all levels of baseball. From Major League ballparks to neighborhood sandlots across the country, Rawlings is everywhere baseball is played.

With more patent designs, cosmetic innovations, and material introductions than any other brand in the marketplace, Rawlings continues to adhere to the ideals on which its founders built the company.

As the exclusive supplier of baseballs to Major League Baseball since 1977 and the official baseball of Minor League Baseball, the NCAA College World Series, the World Baseball Classic, and more than 100 collegiate conferences and youth sport organizations, Rawlings baseballs are integral to the game itself.

By focusing on the elite players at critical defensive positions, Rawlings continuously attracts Gold Glove–caliber players to its advisory staff every year, including 14 out of 18 Rawlings Gold Glove Award Winners in 2016. This continues the annual trend of Rawlings leading all glove brands in Rawlings Gold Glove Award winners year after year, including Hall of Famers such as 16-time winner Brooks Robinson, Ozzie Smith (13 wins), Roberto Clemente (12), Keith Hernandez (11), Johnny Bench (10), and Mike Schmidt (10).

LOOKING AHEAD
Since the company's inception in 1887, Rawlings' mission has always centered on enabling participation by developing and producing innovative, high-performance, and protective equipment and apparel for the professional player. With its comprehensive product portfolio, headlined by its world-renowned fielders' gloves, baseballs, and protective headwear, Rawlings leads the baseball equipment market in the United States with innovations that continue to set the benchmark by which the industry is measured.

Rawlings dominates market share both on-field and at retail, with modern-day stars like Bryce Harper, Kris Bryant, Max Scherzer, and Mike Trout choosing Rawlings and continuing the legacy of elite, next-level athletes demanding the best equipment to reach their peak on-field performance. Rawlings' player-preferred, on-field brand dominance translates directly to the register as Rawlings holds a commanding market-share lead in fielders' gloves, baseballs, and protective headwear across all price points.

The commitment to professional excellence and athletic protection serves as the heart of Rawlings' five brand pillars: Authenticity, Innovation, Performance, Protection, and Professional.

▶ Classic Facts & Anecdotes

- Rawlings started as a sporting goods retail store in St. Louis in 1887 before transitioning to the global manufacturing brand it is today.

- Rawlings developed the first-ever football shoulder pads in 1902, with later models designed by J. W. Heisman — the same Heisman whose name is associated with the trophy awarded to the nation's best collegiate football player.

- Dr. James Naismith, founding father of basketball, designed the first models of Rawlings basketballs in the 1920s.

- Rawlings created one of the first home gyms during World War I with the Rawlings Whitely Exerciser, a system of elastic cords running over pulleys.

- Toronto shortstop and Rawlings Gold Glove Award–winner Troy Tulowitzki named one of his dogs "Rawlings."

See's CANDIES.

THE MARKET

People of all ages love their sweets. More than just a tasty treat, candy is often a welcomed pick-me-up, a wonderful gift, a little piece of happy™. In fact, even when money is tight, candy is an indulgence many are not willing to give up.

Small wonder, then, that despite a stressed economy and increases in commodity costs, including cocoa and sugar, the global candy manufacturing industry has continued to grow.

ACHIEVEMENTS

After opening its first shop in 1921, See's Candies quickly developed a reputation for making unusually high-quality, delicious candy. Customers waited in lines around the block just for a taste. Because of this buzz, See's grew steadily, opening 12 shops by the mid-1920s — and 30 more shops during the Great Depression. Today, the California-based mainstay has over 200 retail shops along with a thriving ecommerce site to satisfy chocolate fans around the world.

The brand's biggest achievement, however, may actually have come in the form of a 7,003-pound chocolate treat. In the summer of 2012, See's made history by setting the Guinness World Record for largest lollipop with its 16-foot, seven-inch confection. This supersized moment was happily shared with over 1 million Facebook fans.

HISTORY

Mary See and her homemade recipes were the inspiration behind See's Candies. But it was her son, Charles A. See, who helped take Mary's confections from beyond the walls of her black-and-white kitchen and into the homes of candy lovers everywhere. After moving his mother and family from Canada to California,

Charles found a financial backer and opened the first See's Candies shop in Los Angeles.

With plenty of competition on the market, Charles knew he needed a key differentiator to make his product special. From the beginning, he decided that distinction would be quality — from the recipes, which would be his mother's, to the ingredients, which would only be the finest.

Customers discovered that See's Candies tasted as good as, if not more delicious than, homemade candy. Better yet, prices were affordable. Even during World War II — when sugar, butter, and cream were in extremely short supply — the company found a way to uphold its commitment to quality. The solution was simple. The best ingredients would still be used, but See's would make less candy. The shops were given a quota, and when the candy ran out, the shops would close until they received additional candy to sell.

For the next 30 years, See's Candies flourished — so much so that the company caught the eye of legendary investor Warren Buffett. From his first bite, Buffett was a fan. He also greatly respected the company's business ethics and quality standards. Thus, in 1972 he and Charlie Munger agreed to bring See's Candies into the Berkshire Hathaway fold. The price was $25 million — a truly sweet investment.

THE PRODUCT

See's makes over 100 different candies, from chocolates and fudge to lollypops (See's spells it with a "y"), bon bons, and brittles. Many of the treats are available year-round, but special seasonal pieces are also featured during the holidays, like the ever-popular handmade, hand-decorated eggs for Easter, creamy Pumpkin Pie Truffles for Thanksgiving, and Scotchmallow® Trees for Christmas.

Mary See's original recipes are still used for some of the most beloved products, including Victoria Toffee and Peanut Brittle. But for new products, See's relies on its resident candy scientist to create these flavors. When developing a new product, See's prefers to come up with treats people can enjoy for generations, shying away from trends or fads. The process is extensive and time-consuming as every element must be refined to perfection; flavor, color, texture, and even how the product will be shipped are all carefully scrutinized.

When manufacturing its candy, See's uses only the very best ingredients available, always eschewing added preservatives. Two California-based candy kitchens churn out up to 1 billion pieces of candy each year, with modern machines

and dedicated employees working side by side. An automated chocolate waterfall coats the candy, and conveyors move the pieces along. Meanwhile, nuts are sorted by hand for quality. Rocky Road is hand-mixed. And every box is carefully packed by hand. The mix of technology and tradition is unique and wonderful.

RECENT DEVELOPMENTS

For most of its 96 years, See's has had the good fortune of making candy so tasty, it practically sells itself. Little marketing and advertising effort was ever needed. Loyalty and recognition on the West Coast have historically been nonissues for See's, since virtually everyone either grew up with the candy or is familiar with the brand. But venture east, and it's a different story.

As See's continues to expand its retail presence into uncharted territory, new challenges and opportunities have emerged. Targeting new markets requires reaching customers who have never heard of or — more importantly — never tasted See's Candies. Facing this dilemma, the company believed the time was ripe to refine the brand experience.

As part of this effort, See's recently developed a new brand book and style guide to move the company from old-fashioned to timeless, from just plain sweet to sweet . . . with a wink. Catalogs, ads, emails, shop signs, flyers, and every other customer touch-point have all been refreshed to reflect the new vision and voice. What See's did not change, and never will, are its core values of taste, quality, tradition, and service.

PROMOTION

Every person who visits a See's Candies shop is offered a piece of candy to try. This long-standing tradition makes it easy for customers to explore flavors they've never tasted before or to enjoy established favorites. Those who know See's will often make a special detour when out shopping just for this daily treat.

To bring in new customers, the company finds creative ways to introduce

people to its delectable confections through fun local events. One such event was held in the middle of New York's Times Square, with a piece of giant 3-D sidewalk art featuring See's lollypops. Free lollypops were handed out to the crowd, and everyone was invited to snap photos of the street art and share their experience via social media.

During peak holiday periods, See's promotes its seasonal products through print and online campaigns, featuring enticing imagery that is clean and simple, letting the candy speak for itself. Most recently, and for the first time in company history, See's began offering free shipping for online and catalog orders — which, to no surprise, was well received by customers.

BRAND VALUES

Everything See's is, and everything See's does, connects to the customer. The company's brand values — taste, quality, tradition, and service — are the basis for its success. Taste creates devoted customers; quality, satisfied customers; tradition, loyal customers; and service, happy customers. It's a simple formula, but one that See's has wholeheartedly followed from day one.

THINGS YOU DIDN'T KNOW ABOUT SEE'S CANDIES

○ Mary See was real, born September 15, 1854. Her own black-and-white kitchen inspired the design of the See's Candies shops.

○ See's is one of the few remaining manufacturers that ages its chocolate. Aging the chocolate results in a smoother, more mellow flavor that's unique to See's.

○ The famously funny *I Love Lucy* episode "Job Switching" was inspired by the See's factory in Los Angeles.

○ Many See's employees have been at the company for 20, 30, 40, even 50 years. They feel See's is like family.

○ Everyone who visits a shop is offered a yummy piece of candy, resulting in over 1 million pounds of candy given away each year.

HISTORY

The story of Sun-Maid begins in the late 1800s in California's great San Joaquin Valley. The saying goes that agriculture was California's "second gold rush." After the 1849 California gold rush drew throngs to the area, people realized that the central valley of California, with its rich soil and Mediterranean climate, was ideally suited for growing fruits of all kinds — and raisins in particular.

In 1912 a group of farmers founded the California Associated Raisin Company, a cooperative financed by small family farmers as well as the Fresno business community, to handle the processing, sales, marketing, and financing necessary to expand raisin consumption throughout the United States and around the world. The new organization was intended to combat low prices and fluctuating demand, and to provide better economies of scale in processing, selling, and creating stable markets. The

organization changed its name to Sun-Maid Growers of California in 1922 to identify more closely with its nationally recognized brand.

During the 1920s renowned artist Norman Rockwell created a series of advertisements that illustrated Sun-Maid's integral place in the traditional American household. These illustrations appeared in the leading magazines of the time, including the *Saturday Evening Post, Good Housekeeping,* and the *Ladies' Home Journal.* Painted in 1927, Rockwell's *In a*

Wonderful Bargain Bag features Sun-Maid's blue "Market Day Special" bag.

Sun-Maid remains a cooperative to this day, owned and operated for the benefit of the 750 family farmers who produce raisins. Some are fourth- or fifth-generation Sun-Maid growers tending grapevines that are 100 years old.

The production method for raisins has not changed much since those early years. In fact, making raisins today could not be simpler or more natural. In September, the ripened grapes are cut from the vines and laid on clean paper trays right on the vineyard floor. Temperatures on the trays can reach upward of 140°F. For dried-on-the-vine harvesting, the canes are cut to allow hanging grapes to dry slowly in the sun. The intense solar energy caramelizes the sugars, giving California raisins their distinct flavor and texture. Once the raisins are dried — after about three weeks — they are delivered to the Sun-Maid processing plant to be washed, sorted, and packaged.

About half of Sun-Maid raisins are packaged and sold in the familiar consumer packages; the other half are marketed for use as an ingredient in a wide assortment of food products. Available year-round, raisins are easy to include in a wide variety of food and are the most economical dried fruits available. Found in cereals, breads, cookies, granola bars, candies, and energy snacks, to name just a few uses, the raisin is one of the world's most versatile food ingredients.

ACHIEVEMENTS

In 2012 Sun-Maid reached the century mark. The cooperative has prospered as a result of its tradition of quality, consistency, innovation, and a focus on the consumer. While reaching 100 years itself is a laudable achievement, other accomplishments designate Sun-Maid as the premier raisin and dried-fruit producer in the world and a recognized American icon:

- In the 1990s, Sun-Maid growers were instrumental in developing DOV (dried-on-the-vine) technology that vastly increases yields and protects against losses from rain damage.

- Sun-Maid introduced a digitally animated Sun-Maid Girl in 2006 to much media interest, keeping not only the Sun-Maid Girl but also the brand itself relevant for the next generation of Sun-Maid consumers.

- Consumer demand prompted Sun-Maid to develop a line of organic raisins. Today, more Sun-Maid growers are converting to organic, and new organic growers are joining the cooperative.

- Sun-Maid's appeal to children as a convenient, portable snack is universal. Through special packaging, Sun-Maid has promoted a number of popular movies, books, DVDs, and TV shows.

- Sun-Maid offers a full line of products, including raisins and other dried fruits, chocolate- and yogurt-covered dried fruits, raisin breads, and bakery items. Sun-Maid also offers its products in bulk as ingredients for food manufacturers.

Sun-Maid has gone green right from the start. As its "Just Grapes & Sunshine" motto says, producing Sun-Maid raisins and dried fruits is an almost completely natural process. More than 90 percent of California natural raisins — 2.5 billion pounds of grapes — are dried by the September sun. Other sustainable practices are as follows:

- Paper tray recycling eliminates much of the burning of paper trays following harvest.

- Water used in the raisin-cleaning process is reused to irrigate forage for cattle.

- All suppliers of corrugated materials are SFI (Sustainable Forestry Initiative)-certified.

- In 2013, Sun-Maid Growers became a registered SmartWay Transport Partner, the US Environmental Protection Agency's flagship program to improve fuel efficiency and reduce greenhouse gases.

LEGACY

No image personifies the healthy, wholesome nature of California sun-dried raisins better than that of the pretty girl whose likeness dons every package of Sun-Maid raisins. With her simple red bonnet, basket of grapes, and smiling face, the Sun-Maid Girl's image can be found on hundreds of millions of raisin packages located on grocery store shelves and in kitchen pantries throughout the United States and in 50 countries around the world. The

significance of her simplicity cannot be overstated, because raisins are simple, natural fuel made from just grapes and sunshine.

Many people want to know if the original Sun-Maid Girl was based on a real person. The

answer is yes, and her name was Lorraine Collett. She originally worked for Sun-Maid as a company representative with several other young women at the Panama Pacific International Exposition in San Francisco in 1915. While back in her hometown of Fresno — the location of Sun-Maid's original headquarters — a Sun-Maid executive saw Lorraine wearing a red bonnet in her backyard and asked her to pose for the painting that would later become the Sun-Maid logo.

In 1915 the association began using the Sun-Maid brand name and the painting of Lorraine Collett. The original Sun-Maid Girl was modified for the first time in 1923, giving her a bigger smile and the image brighter colors and a stylized sun. This more contemporary look kept her in style with the rapidly changing 1920s. In 1956 the trademark was updated for the second time. The sun was moved off-center, intensifying the effect of the sunshine, with the bonnet casting a shadow across the Sun-Maid Girl's face. Brighter colors and a geometric sun modernized the logo's third update in 1970, with the brand's name printed in yellow, giving a warmer, sunnier feel.

The Sun-Maid Girl is a dominant part of the brand's link with consumers. In celebration of her 90th birthday, the Sun-Maid Girl came to life in 2006, which included animating her iconic red bonnet, as well as her surroundings, including a vineyard of raisin grapes. Launched with a full-page ad in *USA Today* and on the Sun-Maid website, the Sun-Maid Girl aired on television with the marketing campaign "Just Grapes & Sunshine" to highlight raisins' natural goodness.

While the animated Sun-Maid Girl helped bring raisins into the information age, she was not designed to replace the Sun-Maid logo. The logo, which has remained the same since 1970, appears on packaging for Sun-Maid products, while the animated Sun-Maid Girl appears on advertising, the Sun-Maid website, and social media. As a brand icon, she is as relevant today as she was 100 years ago — representing wholesomeness and good nutrition to moms and Millennials.

LOOKING AHEAD

The future holds tremendous opportunity for raisins and dried fruits, which grow best in a limited number of unique climates and easily travel the globe to satisfy customers. Today's mobile and globalized environment allows Sun-Maid to link customers around the world with whatever they want to know about growing practices, sustainability, product specifications, nutritional information, and the most enticing raisin and dried fruit recipes for every culture and celebration.

As an ingredient in a favorite recipe or a snack eaten right out of the box, Sun-Maid raisins align with today's top food trends. Raisins are 100 percent non-GMO fruit with no artificial ingredients, no added sugar, no fat, no salt, and no gluten. Making Sun-Maid raisins a part of a healthy diet is a message that has resonated for over a century. As consumers look for foods that are higher in nutritional value and made from simple, recognizable ingredients, Sun-Maid raisins deliver today, just as they've done for more than a century.

Classic Facts and Anecdotes

- The red bonnet worn by Lorraine Collett when she posed for her famous portrait was donated to the Smithsonian Institution in Washington, DC, in 1988.

- More than half of all Sun-Maid raisins are made from green Thompson Seedless grapes, a variety brought to California by English immigrant William Thompson in the 1870s— all from one vine that survived after a devastating spring flood wiped out the rest of Thompson's new crop.

- It takes nearly four and a half pounds of fresh grapes to make one pound of raisins.

TATA CONSULTANCY SERVICES

THE MARKET

Tata Consultancy Services (TCS) is one of the world's top four IT services and consulting organizations, leveraging a comprehensive portfolio of business solutions and the latest digital technologies on behalf of many of the world's largest enterprises — to simplify, strengthen, and transform their businesses. It provides the industry's highest level of certainty and satisfaction through a deep-set commitment to its clients, its comprehensive industry expertise, and an unrivaled global network of delivery centers and innovation labs.

TCS has been recognized by Brand Finance, the world's leading brand valuation firm, as one of the "World's Top Three IT Services and Consulting Organizations," and the fastest-growing brand in the industry over the past seven years. TCS has $16.5 billion in revenue — as of March 31, 2016 — and 378,000 of the sector's best-trained computer scientists, engineers, programmers, data analysts, designers, and more, representing over 129 nationalities via operations in 45 countries. Collectively, TCS is helping its clients to successfully navigate an unprecedented period of disruption and transformation across sectors, from banking and financial services, manufacturing, insurance, and health care, to retail, telecom, hospitality, media and information, and life sciences.

In the United States, TCS has a third of the Fortune 500 brands as customers, is the top

recruiter of local IT services talent over the past three years, and is recognized as a top employer through a broad range of prestigious industry awards. Moreover, TCS is a leading proponent of STEM (science, technology, engineering, and mathematics) education and a significant supporter of health and wellness through its title sponsorship of the TCS New York City Marathon and technology sponsorship of the Chicago and Boston Marathons.

ACHIEVEMENTS

In 2016 TCS was ranked 66th in *Forbes'* "World's 100 Most Innovative Companies" report and featured in the Dow Jones Sustainability Index, a global tracker of the leading sustainability-driven companies. TCS was also ranked in 2016 by Brand Finance as the 58th-most valuable brand in America, across all brands and industries.

Today, women represent nearly 35 percent of TCS' 378,000-member global workforce, making it one of the world's largest private-sector employers of female STEM talent.

While TCS is headquartered in India, the US market represents more than 50 percent of TCS' global business, and the company has called America home for more than 40 years, with operations across the country. TCS' status as the number-one recruiter of American talent in the IT services sector, coupled with its global talent base, has led to TCS frequently being recognized in the HR sector for its impact on the American economy and receiving numerous awards, such as being named the Top Employer in North America for the second consecutive year by the Top Employers Institute.

TCS is also very active in the United States in its commitment to corporate social responsibility. For example, in March 2017, TCS, in partnership with Discovery Education, launched "Ignite My Future in Schools," to engage 20,000 US teachers and one million K–12 students by embedding computer science and computational thinking into core subjects such as math, English, and science. TCS also helped Million Women Mentors — an initiative dedicated to increasing access to STEM education for girls and young women in underserved communities — far exceed its goal by reaching 1.8 million pledges in only three years. As a cofounder and the tech platform provider, it was saluted, alongside other partners, by 20 US senators and congresswomen.

Moreover, specific to health and wellness, TCS became the title sponsor of the TCS New York City Marathon in 2014, and the first-ever

premier and year-round partner of the New York Road Runners (NYRR). Continuing to enhance the race experience through technology, the 2016 marathon witnessed a record 317,000 downloads of the official race app, created by TCS, and was featured as a top free app by Apple on race day.

HISTORY
Established in India in 1968 TCS has grown to its current position as one of the largest IT services firms in the world on the basis of its outstanding customer service record, collaborative partnerships, innovation, and corporate social responsibility.

TCS worked with its first American clients in 1974 and opened its first office in New York City in 1979. Today, TCS has 20 facilities in the United States, and its customer relationships span almost all 50 states, as well as the District of Columbia and Puerto Rico.

TCS is proud of its heritage as part of the Tata Group, founded by Jamsetji Tata in 1868 and one of India's most respected institutions. In fact, 66 percent of the Tata Group's profits are dedicated to philanthropic trusts.

THE PRODUCT
TCS offers a consulting-led, integrated portfolio of IT, digital transformation, business process services (BPS), infrastructure, engineering, and assurance services spanning a diverse range of industries. A deep-set commitment to customers defines how TCS does business. Its unique global engagement model allows customers to

choose the strategy best suited to their business needs. TCS' Innovation Labs, Co-innovation Networks, and Global Delivery Centers (recognized as the global IT services industry benchmark) enable TCS to provide integrated solutions that help businesses quickly recognize value by reducing costs and improving business agility.

RECENT DEVELOPMENTS
In the summer of 2015 TCS launched the world's first cognitive software platform for large enterprises. Named ignio™, it uses machine learning to automate and optimize IT operations and processes within an enterprise, being contextually aware of its working environment and able

to maintain complex software and hardware installations. ignio™ can also monitor the running of the installations, solve problems, analyze the impact of change, and recommend possible solutions — with minimal human intervention. To date, several large enterprise customers have deployed ignio™ or are testing the platform.

Other recent examples of TCS' investments in digital technologies include the launch of a User Experience Center of Excellence and Innovation Lab in Cincinnati, Ohio, in late 2014. And in early 2016 TCS inaugurated a state-of-the-art digital reimagination studio in Santa Clara, California, designed to help customers and partners rapidly ideate bold new innovations and build industry-changing concepts — by leveraging the best of world-class creative, design, engineering, and business domain experts. In fact, almost 15 percent of TCS' revenue now comes from digital offerings — leveraging a combination of cloud computing, big data and analytics, mobility and pervasive computing, social media, and artificial intelligence and robotics — and nearly 190,000 TCS employees were trained and certified in cutting-edge digital technologies to date.

At the grassroots level in North America, TCS' flagship goIT program has expanded to 45 cities (27 in the United States and 18 in Canada). goIT now provides 10,000-plus US and Canadian students with in-school and out-of-school career awareness workshops, hands-on technology and design theory education, and teacher/educator trainings — aimed at getting more students interested in STEM-related careers. Furthermore, TCS was again a cosponsor of the STEM Mentoring Awards at the White House in the summer of 2016.

TCS also marked a new era of partnerships between leaders in industry and academia in 2015, by donating $35 million to Carnegie Mellon University. Representing the largest ever corporate gift to CMU, this donation is funding TCS Hall, a new 48,000-square-foot facility, to support education and joint CMU/TCS cutting-edge research into cognitive computing and autonomous vehicles. The $35 million also supports TCS Presidential Fellowships and Scholarships,

increasing the availability of a CMU education to outstanding students.

PROMOTION
TCS is proud to be the title sponsor of the most prestigious endurance running event in the world: the TCS New York City Marathon. TCS' year-round partnership with NYRR involves significant involvement in a dozen races, such as the half-marathon in Manhattan, where TCS makes the official race app, to being the official partner of NYRR's Youth and Community Services and Track & Field series.

Within two years of this eight-year partnership, NYRR and TCS have worked closely to make the TCS New York City Marathon the most technically advanced and socially engaged marathon in the world. And through its core focus on inspiring family and youth exercise, TCS is also the technology sponsor of the Boston and Chicago Marathons.

BRAND VALUES
Two things stand out at TCS, above all others, specific to its values and culture. First is an unwavering devotion to excellence in customer service, as recognized by its tremendous growth among existing customers, who continue to expand working relationships in America. Second is TCS' deep investment and advocacy of worthy CSR programs. For example, its primary contribution is the dedicated involvement and frequent volunteering of its employees. In 2016 alone, more than 15,000 employees in the United States and Canada volunteered almost 42,000 hours for social good.

THINGS YOU DIDN'T KNOW ABOUT TATA CONSULTANCY SERVICES

❍ In 2013 TCS launched the world's first all-female Business Process Services center in the Kingdom of Saudi Arabia, in collaboration with General Electric (GE) and Saudi Aramco.

❍ As of December 31, 2016, TCS has applied for 3,161 patents. To date, it has been granted 440 patents.

HISTORY

Legend says that the origin of drinking tea dates back to 2737 BC, where it is rumored that Chinese emperor Shen Nung was sitting under a large tea plant (*Camellia sinensis*) while his servant boiled drinking water. Some leaves from the tea plant blew into the water, and an accidental infusion happened, giving birth to the very first cup of tea. However, not until 1660 did sailors bring tea to London coffee shops from China.

When Catherine of Braganza married King Charles II in 1662, she soon established tea as a drink for nobles. Tea was shortly seen as an expensive commodity for the wealthy, and traded as such. In 1664 the East India Company placed its first order to import tea to Britain.

A hundred years later, as British colonists settled in America, the popularity of tea experienced a boom similar to England's. However, it was not without conflict. Britain's practice of levying high taxes on imported goods — often to finance military operations — outraged the colonists. The Tea Act of 1773 gave the East India Company the right to ship tea directly from China, making it impossible for many American importers to stay in business. This act, along with the bitterness of unfair taxation, drove a band of angry patriots to gather at Griffin's Wharf on December 16, 1773, and engage in an action that would forever be known as the Boston Tea Party. The men, disguised as Native Americans, boarded three East India Company ships, tore open all cargos of tea,

and threw them into Boston Harbor. Similar acts of rebellion followed in other American cities, and patriotic citizens turned from tea to coffee to register their disgust with British rule. This

event, and others like it, would ultimately lead to the Revolutionary War.

At the beginning of the 19th century, brothers Joseph and Edward Tetley founded Joseph Tetley & Co. after several years of successfully selling tea off the back of their pack horse. In 1856 they moved the company to London; eventually the brothers parted ways, and Joseph unveiled the renamed "Joseph Tetley & Co., Wholesale Tea Dealers." In 1871 Tetley took his son Joseph "Junior" into partnership, which is when the company began to add blending and packing into its services.

Due to a happy accident, tea bags were born in 1908 when a New York tea merchant sent samples in silken bags. Customers mistakenly placed the silken bags with tea into their teapots, and the tea bag was created. The idea of the tea bag reached Britain in 1939, and shortly thereafter the first Tetley tea-bag machines (aka the grey ladies) began producing 40 tea bags a minute for export. However, in 1940, due to World

War II, Britain began rationing food, including tea. It wasn't until 1952 that Britons were able to have unlimited "cuppas" again.

The company took a major step in 1988, forging an agreement with American agents to distribute Tetley Tea throughout the United States.

Today, Tetley USA is owned by the Tata Group, one of India's oldest, largest, and most respected business unions.

ACHIEVEMENTS

Tetley Tea is the second-largest manufacturer of tea bags worldwide and is one of the leading brands in both the United Kingdom and Canada. It is an established major brand within the United States and Australia; in addition, Tetley has a developing presence in France, Poland, and Russia.

Tetley was the first to introduce tea bags into the UK market, and in 1989 it introduced its signature round bag. Designed to fit snugly at the bottom of one's cup or mug, this tea-bag form allows for more tea in each tea bag, enabling a fuller, stronger brew per cup. This market introduction helped grow Tetley's share by approximately 30 percent. In 1997 Tetley continued its growing list of tea innovations with the introduction of its drawstring bags. Created to squeeze every possible drop of flavor into every cup, Tetley drawstring tea bags have become a favorite with lovers of hot tea.

LEGACY

One question that Tetley often receives is why Tetley teas are blended. The answer is that Tetley blends its tea to produce the flavor of "Tetley." When people select a brand of tea, they are selecting a taste they enjoy. Tea is an agricultural product and is influenced by the climate, soil conditions, and other factors and naturally varies from crop to crop. Therefore, Tetley blends its tea to consistently give consumers the great Tetley tea taste the company is so proud to serve.

Tetley is also proud to provide consumers with varieties of tea and tea infusions. Tetley purchases millions of pounds of tea each week for its different blends. These teas come from as many as 35 different countries and as many as 10,000 different estates. Tetley's buyers and blenders are recognized as some of the foremost experts in the world.

LOOKING AHEAD

Tetley's belief is, "A better state of mind begins with a better tea." Tetley values creating the perfect tea, and the perfect tea moments start with the highest-quality teas. In order to ensure that its teas are of optimal flavor, Tetley selects some of the finest fresh-picked tea leaves from plantations around the world.

More importantly, Tetley cares for its workers and is part of the Ethical Tea Partnership (ETP), a noncommercial alliance of 18 international tea packers working together to promote social responsibility in the world tea trade and assuring the ethical sourcing of tea. The ETP is responsible for monitoring the living and working conditions on tea estates and works with the estate owners to ensure that improvements are consistently made.

When an estate chooses not to meet the minimum standards Tetley promotes, Tetley no longer purchases tea from the company.

In addition to its membership in the ETP, Tetley has committed to source all tea from Rainforest Alliance–certified farms — a step the alliance described as an "industry-changing leap." The ETP works with Rainforest Alliance to help estates achieve Rainforest Alliance certification. Tetley's progress on this journey was recognized in 2013, when its parent company, Tata Global Beverages, was awarded a Sustainable Standard-Setter Award.

▶ **Classic Facts & Anecdotes**

- Tetley was the first to introduce the tea bag into the United Kingdom and the United States. When the tea bag was introduced to Britain in 1953, it had already been in the United States for 33 years.

- Tetley Tea Academy taste tests Tetley Tea eight times, the team has over 909 years of experience, and the blenders taste 39,850 cups of tea every week.

- Tetley UK has a Tetley Tea Folk YouTube channel called thetetleyteafolk.

- Tetley has a tea sommelier whose taste buds were insured in 2015 for 1 million Euros.

The New York Times

HISTORY

Henry Jarvis Raymond and George Jones founded *The New-York Daily Times* in 1851. Its exposé of widespread corruption within the Tammany Hall Democratic organization, run by William Marcy "Boss" Tweed, in New York City helped end Tweed's grip on city politics and became a landmark in American journalism.

Adolph S. Ochs, a newspaper publisher from Chattanooga, Tennessee, bought *The Times* in 1896, which was then having severe financial difficulties. He took *The Times* to new heights, establishing it as the serious, balanced newspaper that would bring readers "All the News That's Fit to Print" (a slogan he coined that still appears on the paper's front page). His publication would do so, he added, "without fear or favor." Ochs introduced such features as *The New York Times Magazine* and the *Book Review*.

In 1935 Ochs was succeeded as publisher by his son-in-law, Arthur Hays Sulzberger, whose grandson, Arthur Sulzberger Jr., is the publisher today. With its extensive coverage of world events throughout the 20th century, *The Times* came to be known as "the newspaper of record."

The Supreme Court ruled in favor of the newspaper's right in 1971 to publish the so-called Pentagon Papers, government documents concerning the Vietnam War. In 1996 *The Times* entered the dawning digital era, launching its acclaimed website, NYTimes.com. More than 20 years later, the site has grown significantly, with an array of expanded sections and capabilities, videos, infographics, multimedia, blogs, and more.

ACHIEVEMENTS

Pulitzer Prizes. *The New York Times* has won more Pulitzer Prizes, the most prestigious award in journalism, than any other news organization. At press time, the count was 119.

George Polk Awards. Established by Long Island University in 1949 to memorialize the CBS correspondent slain covering the civil war in Greece, the George Polk Award has become one of America's most coveted journalism honors. *The Times* has earned more than 100 of them.

Gerald Loeb Awards. Intending to encourage reporting on subjects that would both inform and protect the private investor and the general public, Gerald Loeb created these awards in 1957 to honor journalists who make significant contributions to the understanding of business, finance, and the economy. Distinguished journalists nationwide participate. UCLA's Anderson School of Management has presented the

program since 1973. *The Times* has received 15 Gerald Loeb Awards.

Sabew Awards. *The Times* won six Sabew Awards in 2016. Sabew — the Society of American Business Editors & Writers — is an association of business journalists headquartered at the University of Missouri School of Journalism. Competition began in 1995 to help set standards and recognize role models for outstanding business journalism. The intent of the award is to encourage comprehensive reporting of economic events without fear or favoritism.

The Times provides daily news and analysis of the world, nation, and New York area, along with business and sports, the arts, science, technology, and trends. Content from *The Times* is available in its print edition, on the Web at NYTimes.com, and in various digital products and mobile applications.

Climbing and Cloning Sequoias

Time magazine has hailed *The Times* as "easily the best, most important newspaper in the country." *The Times* makes its content available to other national and international customers

and offers consumers photo reprints and other products at *The New York Times* Store (nyt store.com). *The Times* is valued not only for its extensive coverage but also for the careful analysis and authoritative context it provides.

The New York Times on the Web, at NYTimes.com, is one of the most admired and most innovative — as well as the most visited — newspaper websites. It includes widely discussed blogs on every subject, videos, columns, multimedia graphics, and slide shows, as well as archives of past articles.

LEGACY

The New York Times is one of the world's most honored and trusted news sources, building on a tradition of full, balanced, authoritative news coverage that goes back more than 160 years.

The Times is both the nation's largest seven-day newspaper and the number-one newspaper website. Industry leaders nationwide who are seeking — from a single source — the most complete, compelling, and thoughtful reporting on news and trends read *The Times*. Marketers in all categories place their ads in *The Times*, on NYTimes.com, and on various *Times* mobile products to reach loyal and influential readers, discerning consumers, and decision makers in business, government, and other fields.

LOOKING AHEAD

The Times has a long-standing reputation for integrity and depth of reporting. Readers value *The Times* because they know it provides all the most important news, as well as highly respected insights. In an era of ever-growing media choices, readers rely on *The Times* for accuracy, substance and style, range and depth.

Advertisers value *The Times* for the closely read, highly esteemed, and timely editorial environment in which their messages will appear, and because of the influence and purchasing power of so many *Times* readers.

The Times extends its brand awareness through TimesTalks, live panel discussions involving *Times* journalists, as well as its live conference series, with events such as DealBook and Energy for Tomorrow.

▶ Classic Facts & Anecdotes

- Times Square was named for *The New York Times* after the paper moved to the neighborhood in 1905. Previously the area was known as Longacre Square.

- The first Times Square New Year's Eve ball dropped from The Times Tower on December 31, 1907. One hundred years later, in 2007, *The Times* moved into a new headquarters building, designed by Renzo Piano, at Eighth Avenue between 40th and 41st Streets.

- *The New York Times* was the first newspaper to publish an accurate story about the sinking of the *Titanic* in 1912.

- The first Sunday crossword appeared in *The New York Times Magazine* in 1942. The first crossword in the daily paper appeared in 1950.

- *The Times* first popularized the Op-Ed page, which it introduced in 1970, running opinion pieces by outside writers on the page opposite its editorials: hence, "Op-Ed."

- TimesMachine is an online resource that allows readers to flip electronically through any issue from volume 1, number 1 of *The New-York Daily Times,* on September 18, 1851, through *The New York Times* of December 30, 1922.

THE MARKET

United Van Lines, as part of the UniGroup family of companies, is uniquely positioned to serve the more than 15 million American households moving annually and the millions more moving worldwide. In addition to moving personal household goods, United also provides transportation and logistics services to companies around the world.

United is America's #1 Mover®, offering single-source control and embracing common quality standards throughout the world for residential moves and the corporate transportation needs of its customers. Because of United's notable agency footprint, its customers can expect to be served by qualified professionals, no matter where they are located throughout the world.

United's agency family is more than just branches of a larger organization; United agents are "customer service centers" whose work is geared toward exceeding customers' expectations. United's quality commitment is not only for its household goods services; it also extends into specialized logistics services. From intricate trade show exhibits and delicate store fixtures to sensitive medical equipment and priceless fine art, United has the expertise and experience to successfully manage and transport whatever the specialized shipment may be.

ACHIEVEMENTS

United is proud to offer its moving customers a variety of services in addition to moving and storage that add value to the overall relocation process and can ultimately save the customer money. With the CityPointe program, customers receive access to data on metropolitan areas throughout North America, including demographics, climate, crime, education, health care, and housing. Because buying and selling a home are typically the most expensive and challenging aspects of relocation, choosing a professional real estate agent can be an enormous asset. United assists its customers with finding real estate agents both at the current and future home locations, and the customer may be eligible to receive cash back as part of this process. Selecting the right mortgage lender can help customers save time and money. Through United's preferred relationships, customers can secure the financing for their new homes while managing their costs and schedule. They receive the benefit of working with a lender who understands relocation as well as access to preapprovals, buydowns, and closing specials that may be available.

Additionally, United offers its customers a number of services through its trusted partners

to help its customers settle in to their new homes faster. From computer and home theater setup to maid service, United's Straight Talk Advantage settling-in services help families make their new house a home.

HISTORY

The concept that evolved into United Van Lines originated in 1928 when Return Loads Service Inc. was formed in Cleveland, Ohio, to arrange return shipments for independent moving companies transporting goods from one city to another. Orders were centrally registered and dispatched, and certificates of membership were sold to independent moving companies, which paid a revenue percentage on every order handled.

The premise of Return Loads Service Inc. was to enable movers, once they had delivered a shipment, to obtain profitable tonnage to haul on the return trip instead of operating an empty van. When similar return shipment companies began appearing around the country, the Cleveland firm adopted the distinctive title of United Van Service. The Depression spelled disaster for the fledgling firm, as United found itself unable to keep up service with depleted revenues, and many agents broke away to operate independently. In June 1933 United Van Service was dissolved, and its assets and liabilities were transferred to a new entity incorporated as United Van Lines. The new firm prospered and, in 1936, moved its headquarters to St. Louis.

In 1947 the ownership of United Van Lines passed from the few original stockholders who held the firm together during its formative stages to a larger group of United agents, establishing the structure that has remained intact for more than six decades.

To support United agents in the transportation business, the corporation has created related operating companies that sell and lease equipment needed by the moving industry, and provide global mobility management services. These operating entities are overseen by UniGroup, a holding company formed in 1988 and owned by UniGroup companies' affiliated agents and senior management.

moving and storage solutions, from full-service to do-it-yourself with portable containers that customers can pack and load themselves.

United's approach to the evolving operating environment has consistently been characterized by a commitment to quality — to the importance of the individual's investment of excellence in a service or product to make it discernibly better than that of the competition.

In 2003 United became ISO certified, and the company is currently ISO 9001:2008 certified, proving its commitment to quality.

United's superior performance is verified by consumer surveys and an even more telling gauge: repeat business. United moves more than just people and their belongings. Whether it's down the street or to the other side of the globe, the company offers worldwide specialized logistics solutions for high-value products, trade shows, and other special commodities. Since 1959 it has been providing specialized transportation services, each year delivering more than a quarter of a million specialized shipments.

RECENT DEVELOPMENTS
During its Annual Education Conference & Expo in March 2016, the American Moving & Storage Association (AMSA) presented United Van Lines with its 2015 Fleet Safety Award in the over 50 million miles category. AMSA presents the award to recognize moving and storage companies for their overall safety, creativity, and leadership in safety program design.

"Safety is a top priority for United Van Lines," said United Van Lines director of safety Dave Pile. "We stay on top of the latest rules, trends, and technology to make continuous improvements to our safety programs and are honored that AMSA recognized these ongoing efforts."

PROMOTION
For more than 30 years, United Van Lines has released its annual migration study showing which states the moving public is leaving and where they are going. Journalists, researchers, and experts rely on this data to give them important trend information about the migration of the US population. The United Van Lines study was the first of its kind and continues to be mentioned in publications and in broadcasts across the country each year.

BRAND VALUES
United's quality and professionalism set it apart from other movers. As America's #1 Mover, United has the innovative services and expertise to serve every customer, from do-it-yourself to full-service moving and storage. United's commitment to quality has been the focus of its taglines throughout the years. Beginning in 1948 the tag was "Moving with Care . . . Everywhere," which showed United's commitment to quality and global thinking. Changing the slogan to represent United's focus on the customer, a new line — "Even Our Name Begins With You" — came out in 1978. In the 1980s society was looking for a simple answer to all its needs. United responded with its tagline "The Total Transportation Company," conveying that it was a one-stop resource for all of its customers' needs. A more recent slogan, "The Quality Shows In Every Move We Make," focuses once again on United's commitment to quality.

THINGS YOU DIDN'T KNOW ABOUT UNITED VAN LINES

○ United Van Lines is the United States' largest household goods mover.

○ United Van Lines is recognized as the nation's leading corporate transportation provider, with half of the Fortune 500 companies and more than 5,000 corporate account customers using its services.

THE PRODUCT
The moving industry is a people business, and United's devotion to this premise is reflected in the quality services it provides, as well as the strong ties it readily forms and maintains with large corporations and individual moving customers. United knows that no two customers are alike, which is why it provides a full range of

VANHEUSEN

HISTORY

The *Van Heusen* story dates back to 1881 in Pottsville, Pennsylvania, when Moses Phillips, along with his wife, Endel, first began mending and then selling shirts for local coal miners. After achieving success in this limited market, the business moved beyond mending, and at the suggestion of his son Isaac, Moses Phillips moved the operations to New York City. The move signified a transition of the business from small town to the national stage.

In New York, looking for a partner to exploit his patented soft-folding collar process, John M. van Heusen met with Isaac Phillips, who bought the patent, and the Phillips–*Van Heusen*, or PVH, alliance was born. Due largely to the success of the Van Heusen *"World's Smartest Collar,"* the family business continued to develop and expand to what it is today.

The ongoing success of the *Van Heusen* brand can be attributed to a commitment to provide customers with quality products and innovative marketing.

America's number-one dress shirt brand, *Van Heusen*, has been associated with stylish, affordable, and high-quality dress shirts since the introduction of the patented *Van Heusen* "soft-folding" collar in 1921. This innovation only added to the fabled history of its manufacturer, Phillips-Jones Company Inc., a shirt company with a history that dated back to 1881. The *Van Heusen* brand has had remarkable success throughout the world — particularly in the United States, where it has been the best-selling dress shirt brand in department and chain stores since 1991. Also a leading national brand in the sportswear market, *Van Heusen* has consistently ranked as the best-selling woven sport shirt brand in US department and chain stores.

VAN PARK
A VAN HEUSEN
–PATENTED–
COLLAR 50¢

In 2001 PVH acquired the worldwide rights to the *Van Heusen* trademark, bringing all rights to the brand in-house and allowing PVH to further develop the brand's global reach.

The *Van Heusen* brand has proven strong enough to expand its reach beyond its dress-shirt heritage into successful product lines in men's and women's dress, sportswear, and accessories. Today, *Van Heusen* products are sold in major department and chain stores and *Van Heusen* company-operated stores in the United States, as well as licensee-operated stores outside of the United States. The brand also has international appeal, with approximately 30 licensees covering approximately 85 territories worldwide in product categories including men's, women's. and children's formalwear, sportswear, and accessories.

ACHIEVEMENTS

As America's leading dress shirt brand, *Van Heusen* has become synonymous with men's style. With a strong foundation in men's dress furnishings, *Van Heusen* ranked as America's number-one best-selling national brand dress shirt across US department and chain stores in 2015. Products are primarily distributed in North America through department stores and in approximately 170 company-operated *Van Heusen* outlet stores in the United States and Canada.

The *Van Heusen* brand engages loyal consumers and grows its audience by promoting the brand in ways that resonate with its consumer base. The "*Van Heusen* Institute of Style" campaign, launched in 2011, featured NFL Hall of Famers Steve Young and Jerry Rice as "Professors of Style," a successful multimedia campaign that brought football heroes into people's living rooms

to provide tips on fashion. The "*Van Heusen* Institute of Style" campaign eventually expanded to include television, print, digital, and social media, and collaborated with the Funny or Die website for a special "Institute of Style" video.

Van Heusen's Flex Collar line features a collar that can expand an extra half inch, keeping men feeling great all day. The fabric for the collar is taken and compacted far beyond the range of normal shrinkage. A stretching device is then incorporated into the collar band, allowing it to expand seamlessly — always returning to its original position and providing maximum comfort for the wearer. The flexible collar also flares to accommodate wider tie knots.

LEGACY

Not content to lead the market with product alone, *Van Heusen* has long been an innovator in apparel marketing and promotion. In the 1950s *Van Heusen* became one of the first companies in the world to use celebrities to endorse its brand. Mickey Rooney, Anthony Quinn, Tony Curtis, Bob Hope, Jerry Lewis, Burt Lancaster, Jimmy Stewart, and future president Ronald Reagan all served as spokesmen for *Van Heusen* dress shirts.

Van Heusen was also one of the first apparel brands with advertising at sports stadiums, adorning outfield walls at both Ebbets Field and Yankee Stadium.

LOOKING AHEAD

PVH continues to invest in *Van Heusen*'s core dress and sport shirt products, while expanding into a more comprehensive offering of apparel and accessories for men, women, and children, both through its own retail stores and through licensing the brand around the world.

The men's lines are available in department stores in and outside of the United States, including Canada, India, Australia, Peru, and Chile, as well as in hundreds of *Van Heusen* retail stores around the world. Licensed *Van Heusen* products include dress shirts (outside the US only); sportswear (outside the US only); suits, ties, trousers, and underwear (outside the US only); socks, boys' clothing, jewelry, eyewear, headwear, footwear, and scarves (outside the US only); and gloves, outerwear, loungewear (outside the US only), bags, and small leather goods. The women's apparel lines in the United States are exclusive to PVH's own *Van Heusen* retail stores.

Van Heusen is a 24/7 lifestyle brand known not only for dress shirts but for both men's and women's dresswear, sportswear, and accessories that stand out for their fit, fabric, finish, and innovative fashion — at a fraction of the cost of luxury brands. *Van Heusen* has also emerged as a fashion authority: men and women now look to the brand for expert advice on what to wear, when to wear it, and how to wear it.

▶ Classic Facts and Anecdotes

- The Phillips-Jones Co., now PVH Corp., owner of the *Van Heusen* trademark, produced the first men's sport shirt in 1912.

- During World War II, the US military engaged the Phillips-Jones Co. to produce shirts for US troops.

- Andy Warhol created a screen print in 1985 based on Ronald Reagan's *Van Heusen* Century Shirt ad from 1953.

AECOM

HEATHER RIM
Senior Vice
President,
Chief Marketing
and Communi-
cations Officer

Senior vice president and chief marketing and communications officer for AECOM, Heather Rim is charged with combining the full strength of the firm's global marketing and communications professionals to advance business development opportunities, inspire brand loyalty, and engage employees and the marketplace. Her responsibilities include strategic marketing, brand management, advertising, public relations, corporate social responsibility, employee communications, and digital communications.

Prior to joining AECOM in 2015, Ms. Rim was vice president, global corporate communications, at Avery Dennison, and previously held communications and marketing roles at companies including the Walt Disney Company, WellPoint, Countrywide, and KPMG. A graduate of the University of Southern California and Azusa Pacific University, Ms. Rim also serves on the boards of the United Way of Greater Los Angeles, Downtown Women's Center, and the University of Southern California Center for Public Relations.

AECOM

TARA MCADAM
KASSAL
Vice President,
Global Brand
Strategy

AECOM's vice president of global brand strategy Tara McAdam Kassal leads the development of brand positioning and building of brand equity to achieve market differentiation and drive business growth for the global firm. Prior to this role, Ms. Kassal served as chief marketing officer for Tishman Construction and AECOM's construction services practice, directing teams in market planning, brand building, marketing communications, business development, market research, and win strategies.

Before joining AECOM, Ms. Kassal served as senior vice president of marketing for Lend Lease Americas and led marketing and communications for architecture, planning, and engineering entities, all marked by periods of record growth for the firms. A graduate of Boston University, Ms. Kassal completed postgraduate work at Columbia University and serves as co-chair of the Urban Land Institute's New York District Council Programming Committee.

Arrow

GEOFFREY BARRETT
President,
National Brand
Sportswear

Geoff Barrett is president of national brand sportswear at PVH. In this role, he oversees the wholesale business for Arrow, Van Heusen, Geoffrey Beene, J. Garcia, and G. H. Bass & Co. Within these divisions, Geoff is responsible for sales, planning, design, and merchandising.

Geoff began his career in Baton Rouge, Louisiana, as a buyer in the training program at retailer Gottschalks. In 1984 he followed in the footsteps of his father, Walter, a 35-year top sales veteran, and joined PVH. Geoff started as a sales trainee in Dallas, Texas, and then made lateral moves to New Orleans, Iowa, and Washington, DC. Geoff later relocated to the company's headquarters in New York City, when he became national sales manager of Arrow dress shirts and held various sales management positions with increasing responsibility until becoming president of national sportswear in 2009.

Geoff earned a bachelor of science in marketing from Louisiana State University, which he attended on a swimming scholarship. He is currently a board member at the Madison (New Jersey) Montessori School, Berkeley Aquatic Club, and Chatham Youth Hockey.

AXA Equitable

STEVE D'EREDITA
Vice President, AXA
Equitable Life
Insurance Company

Steve has over 25 years of experience in the insurance and financial services industry. He has managed various life and annuity administrative areas, as well as numerous strategic corporate projects. Steve's areas of expertise include functions of variable annuity contract and life policy administration, policy creation and implementation, call center, customer relationship management, and team building. Steve has responsibilities for AXA Equitable's Retirement Savings Division, which includes overseeing the New Business, Association, and Conservation Departments. Steve also serves as the business continuity site coordinator. Steve is a graduate of State University of New York at Fredonia, is a Series 6 and 26 NASD Registered Principal, and holds the Associate of Customer Service (ACS) and Associate, Insurance Agency Administration (AIAA) professional designations.

Big Brothers Big Sisters

PAM IORIO
President and CEO

Leading Big Brothers Big Sisters of America (BBBSA) is President and CEO Pam Iorio, the former two-term mayor of Tampa, Florida.

Iorio became the leader of BBBSA, the nation's oldest mentoring organization, in March 2014. Today, there are over 300 affiliates in all 50 states matching volunteers, called "Bigs," with children, "Littles." These caring relationships help change a young person's life for the better.

BBBSA is undergoing a nationwide strategic planning process, and recently launched Bigs in Blue, a national initiative to recruit police officers as mentors, building bridges between police and the communities they serve.

Iorio has a B.S. in political science from American University and an M.A. in history from the University of South Florida.

Fedex

MONICA SKIPPER
Managing Director,
Global Brand
Management

Monica Skipper's marketing experience spans nearly three decades and includes database and direct marketing, small business, retail, and global brand management. Today, she serves as the chief brand evangelist for one of the world's most recognized brands, FedEx. Monica is a sought-after public speaker, philanthropist, and creative thinker. She holds an MBA from the University of Memphis and is a regular guest lecturer at Dowling College and the University of Memphis.

Monica is passionate about her community and is active nationally and locally in various organizations. She is the founder and president of Kole's Club, a nonprofit that benefits the families of children at St. Jude Children's Research Hospital. When she is not managing the brand at FedEx, Monica lends her expertise to support other nonprofit brands, such as the American Red Cross, the Church Health Center, and FedExFamilyHouse, supporting Le Bonheur Children's Hospital.

IZOD

MOLLY YEARICK
President,
Izod Retail and
Wholesale

Molly Yearick was appointed to the role of president, Izod Retail and Wholesale, in November 2013. In this role, Molly oversees PVH's retail and wholesale operations under the IZOD brand, including marketing, design, merchandising, and planning.

Prior to that, Molly served as president of Tommy Hilfiger Wholesale North America, in which she managed the design, sales, merchandising, sourcing, and planning teams for men's sportswear and women's sportswear and accessories in the United States and Canada. Molly also served as president of Calvin Klein Sportswear, the company's wholesale men's sportswear division, from June 2006 to February 2011. Molly joined PVH in 2003 as executive vice president of sales and marketing for Calvin Klein Sport.

Prior to arriving at PVH, Molly served as executive vice president of sales for Perry Ellis men's sportswear at Salant Corporation. She began her career in retail in 1985 as a buyer for Robinson's in Los Angeles, moving to New York 10 years later to become vice president of sales at Guess Inc.

Molly graduated from Bucknell University with a bachelor of science in education and math.

Konica Minolta

RICK TAYLOR
President and Chief
Operating Officer

Rick Taylor serves as president and chief operating officer of Konica Minolta Business Solutions U.S.A. Inc. He is responsible for core corporate operations that support all business areas across the United States, including leading the coordination and operation of all corporate business sales and service strategies as well as marketing, administration, finance, legal, and training. Taylor serves on Konica Minolta's Global Strategy Council, addressing worldwide business transformation and growth strategies for Konica Minolta.

Taylor's industry experience is vast in creating new revenue avenues while maintaining a cohesive and productive sales strategy for business partners. In 2008 Taylor joined Konica Minolta from Toshiba America Business Solutions Inc., where he was the company's president and chief executive officer. In the past 10 years, Taylor has been named Executive of the Year six times in a Marketing Research Consultants' survey of independent office equipment dealers.

Konica Minolta

**KEVIN P. KERN
Senior Vice President,
Marketing
Konica Minolta
Business Solutions
U.S.A. Inc.**

With more than 19 years of experience in the office imaging industry, Kevin P. Kern, senior vice president, marketing, oversees all corporate marketing initiatives and is responsible for the planning and development of new products for Konica Minolta Business Solutions U.S.A. Inc.

Previously, Kevin served as legacy Konica's vice president, new product development and support, overseeing the planning and development for all Konica products as well as for the company's Digital Systems Solutions area. Kevin joined Konica Business Technologies Inc. in 1994 as director, product marketing, and was appointed director, marketing, in 1995. Before joining Konica, he was marketing manager for Canon U.S.A. Kevin earned a bachelor of science in business from the University of Massachusetts–Dartmouth.

Kevin and his wife, Nancy, have three children and reside in Orange County, New York. In his spare time, Kevin enjoys playing guitar with his friends and flying airplanes over the northeast corridor of the United States.

Martin Guitars

**CHRISTIAN
FREDERICK
MARTIN, IV
Chairman and Chief
Executive Officer**

C. F. Martin, IV, or "Chris" as he prefers, is the chairman and CEO of the world-renowned C. F. Martin & Co. and the sixth generation of Martin family members to run the business. Under Chris's direction, the company has maintained its integrity and industry-wide respect while growing and prospering to unprecedented manufacturing and sales levels.

Rawlings

**J. MICHAEL
THOMPSON
Executive Vice
President and
General Manager of
Diamond Sports,
Jarden Team Sports**

Now in his 29th year with Jarden Team Sports, Mike Thompson assumed chief marketing duties for all JTS brands in 2009. Starting as a sales representative in 1984 Mike quickly ascended the corporate ladder with promotions from regional sales manager to vice president of sales; Rawlings's sales revenue more than tripled during his tenure. Mike's current responsibilities include managing Jarden Team Sports' diamond sports product development and sports marketing ventures, including Rawlings's partnership with Major League Baseball.

Tata Consultancy Services Limited

**SURYA (SURY)
KANT, President,
North America, UK
and Europe, TCS**

Surya (Sury) Kant, president, North America, UK and Europe, TCS, is responsible for overseeing and strengthening customer relationships and revenues across TCS's largest markets (regions that account for more than 75 percent of the company's global revenues), and plays a key role in expanding the company's range of technology and service offerings. In addition, Sury plays a lead role supporting US STEM education and career initiatives — particularly for women and minorities — through prominent partnerships with the likes of STEMConnector®, Million Women Mentors, US2020, and NPower. He received his bachelor's degree in electrical engineering with a specialization in electronics from Delhi College of Engineering, and his master's degree in electrical engineering with a specialization in computer technology from ITT Delhi.

Tata Consultancy Services Limited

BALAJI GANAPATHY
Head of Workforce
Effectiveness, TCS

Balaji Ganapathy, head of workforce effectiveness, TCS, oversees the functions of corporate social responsibility, diversity and inclusion, and HR Business Consulting. Under his stewardship, TCS is using its technology innovation, thought leadership, and skill-based volunteering to impact the state of STEM education in North America, with a special focus on impacting women and girls, minorities, and underrepresented groups. Balaji serves as the chair of STEMconnector®'s STEM Innovation Task Force, chairperson of NPower's TCC Advisory Council, vice-chair of the Million Women Mentors Leadership Council, Executive Committee of IMPACT 2030, World Economic Forum's Education Steering Committee, and US Chamber of Commerce's Education, Employment, and Training Committee. He is a postgraduate in human resources management and a bachelor of technology in mechanical engineering.

Van Heusen

KENNETH L. WYSE
President of Licensing
and Public Relations

Ken Wyse is the president of licensing and public relations at PVH. Based in the New York City headquarters, Ken is responsible for extending licensing on current brands, creating new opportunities, and directing national and international fashion publicity/promotion for the IZOD, Van Heusen, Bass, and Arrow licensed products.

Ken joined PVH in 1987 as the director of international licensing. He has held roles in licensing, global marketing, and communications. As the SVP of licensing, he was responsible for all domestic and international operations.

Before PVH, Ken was corporate marketing director at Liz Claiborne Inc., vice president of licensing at Bon Jour International, and international managing director at Jordache Enterprises. He began his career at Gulf and Western Industries, where he developed global export strategies for their subsidiaries.

An Ohio native, Ken earned a bachelor's degree in Latin American studies from Union College and then a master's in business administration in international business at Baruch College.

Ken is chairman of the Business Council and member of the Leadership Council of Lincoln Center. He is also chairman of the YMA Youth Mentoring Association / Fashion Scholarship Fund. Ken currently resides in New York City.

AWARDED

America's
Greatest Brands

2017